"Ajayan Borys writes clearly and insightfully about the meaning and practice of meditation, exploring the chakras, the use of mantra, and the healing power of purification. He points out that although spiritual practice requires discipline and effort, the ultimate nature of meditation is uncontrived and effortless. This is a book that will inspire and guide those who seek a more fulfilling and meaningful way of being."

— Shyalpa Tenzin Rinpoche, author of
Living Fully: Finding Joy in Every Breath

"*Effortless Mind* is a pure gift! I loved it! Ajayan Borys is a master meditator who speaks in clear, practical, engaging language to offer a profound program of meditation that anyone can learn. In fact, his book inspires us to embrace meditation more readily than any other work or practice that I have experienced. Most importantly, he reveals how to integrate the benefits of meditation into your daily life and make every moment a meditation. Ajayan is a teacher of the highest caliber. Thanks, Ajayan, for this monumental work. I highly recommend it."

— David Daniels, MD, clinical professor of psychiatry and behavioral sciences, Stanford Medical School, and pioneer in the Enneagram system of nine personality styles

"The following words, spoken by a smiling Himalayan swami to Ajayan Borys, sum up everything I have to say about this book and life: '[People] don't realize that life without meditation is like a string of zeros. But adding meditation is like adding a 1 in front of all those zeros. Now you have a million, or a billion, or a trillion.' The zero in our lives represents the indescribable, the undifferentiated, and the meaningless — the source of life. The 1 is also not an ordinary number, as 1 multiplied or divided by 1 is still 1. Life begins when we create the number 10 by connecting the two through our meditation. And as the swami knew, this is only the beginning. This book can help you to connect with your higher Self and, as a result, with all creation."

— Bernie S. Siegel, MD, author of
A Book of Miracles and *Faith, Hope & Healing*

"Written with the grace and ease of meditation itself, *Effortless Mind* is a balm to the soul. Find herein the keys to the inner temple, a gateway into the deepest mystery, and an antidote to life's stress. If you are looking for a way in instead of a way out, this book is for you."

— Anodea Judith, PhD, author of
Wheels of Life and *Eastern Body, Western Mind*

EFFORTLESS
MIND

EFFORTLESS MIND

MEDITATE WITH EASE

AJAYAN BORYS

New World Library
Novato, California

New World Library
14 Pamaron Way
Novato, California 94949

"Effortless Mind" is a registered trademark of Henry J. Borys (writing as Ajayan Borys).

The material in this book is intended for education. It is not meant to take the place of diagnosis and treatment by a qualified medical practitioner or therapist. No expressed or implied guarantee as to the effects of the use of the recommendations can be given or liability taken.

The techniques taught in this book are unique. No claim is made that they bear any resemblance to the Transcendental Meditation® Program as taught by Maharishi Mahesh Yogi or the Integrated Amrita Meditation Technique® as taught by Mata Amritanandamayi. If you wish to learn those specific techniques, please refer to those organizations.

Excerpt on page 125 from *Verses on the Faith-Mind*, by Hsin-Hsin Ming, translated by Richard B. Clarke, copyright © 1973, 1984, 2001 by Richard B. Clarke. Reprinted with permission of White Pine Press, www.whitepine.org.

Text design by Tona Pearce Myers

Library of Congress Cataloging-in-Publication Data is available.

First printing, February 2013
ISBN 978-1-60868-154-9
Printed in Canada on 100% postconsumer waste-recycled paper

 New World Library is proud to be a Gold Certified Environmentally Responsible Publisher. Publisher certification awarded by Green Press Initiative. www.greenpressinitiative.org

10 9 8 7 6 5 4 3 2 1

For my beloved Keesha, my best friend,
companion, and inspiration,
who showed me that every moment is meditation

Om
Lokah samastah sukhino bhavantu
Lokah samastah sukhino bhavantu
Lokah samastah sukhino bhavantu
Om shanti shanti shanti

May all beings be happy.
Om peace, peace, peace.

CONTENTS

INTRODUCTION

You have probably heard of the many benefits of meditation: deep relaxation, reduced depression and anxiety, increased vitality and mental clarity, improved health, and more. You may also be aware that not only do spiritual teachers recommend meditation, but nowadays even many medical providers prescribe it to their patients. Yet despite the growing enthusiasm for meditation, figuring out where to begin can be confusing. Health professionals may recommend it, but that doesn't change the fact that, for many people, meditation still has an air of mystery about it. So what is meditation, really? How does it work? Even those who take one of the many meditation classes available may wonder: Am I meditating correctly? What is the experience of meditation supposed to feel like? Have I learned a really effective technique, or am I wasting my time?

This book is designed to teach you proven meditation

practices that are simple, easy, and enjoyable, yet so profound that you will have no doubt they are effective. If you follow the instructions given here, you will soon know from your personal experience that you are meditating correctly, because the experience of deep meditation is unmistakable. You will also feel the benefits of meditation in your daily life — inner calm, strength, and peace; increased vitality, creativity, and positive outlook; improved health; and more harmonious and loving relationships. Finally, you will understand what meditation is and what it is not. You will understand how it works and how to handle any experience that may arise during meditation. In other words, you will be ready to embark on your own personal meditation practice.

The good news is that the profound meditation techniques taught in this book are readily accessible and easy to practice. This is true for anyone, whether you're twelve years old or a hundred. The best forms of meditation are effortless, because they are about being, not about doing. Doing requires effort; being is effortless. For this reason, meditation is the easiest thing you'll ever experience — yet it opens you to live what is highest and best in yourself, your true Self, your higher Self.

WHAT IS EFFORTLESS MIND MEDITATION?

A quick Internet search will show that there are many forms of meditation. So why should you choose Effortless Mind? Over the past forty-two years, I've traveled the globe exploring, practicing, and teaching a variety of meditation techniques. Always, during that time, I sought out techniques that are simple to practice and yet deliver the greatest results. Effortless

Mind is the culmination of that exploration. It consists of a balanced program of meditation combining the three highly effective techniques that you will learn in this book:

- CHAKRA MEDITATION. This is a meditation on the primary spiritual centers in the body to awaken higher consciousness and spiritual energy. You will first learn a preliminary exercise and then the three levels of this unique approach to chakra meditation. This will not only vitalize your body and mind but also empower and deepen the meditations that follow.
- MANTRA MEDITATION IN THE HEART CENTER. This is a classical and deeply relaxing meditation that dissolves stress and tension as well as allowing you to traverse all the subtle levels of the mind, awaken intuition and creativity, and open to delicate, blissful layers of feeling.
- MEDITATION FOR HEALTH AND LONGEVITY. This practice infuses your body with the healing power of awareness, bringing health, lightness, and joy.

This may sound like a lot to learn, but as you will see, each aspect of Effortless Mind is simple. Just take it step by step, and by the end of the book you will have easily mastered it all.

HOW TO USE THIS BOOK

For thousands of years, the art of meditation has been passed down from teacher to student. If the teacher is skilled, he or she can bring the student to a state of receptivity where the student can effortlessly experience deep meditation. As we shall see, that effortlessness is the secret to success. It doesn't matter whether you learn to meditate from a teacher in person or from a book: If your practice isn't effortless, it won't be successful. If your practice *is* effortless, it will be successful no matter how you learned it. It's that simple.

Learning meditation from a book is entirely possible. Even the meditations of such great mystics as Saint Teresa of Avila were said to have been first inspired and guided by books. There is only one hitch: When learning from a book, the natural temptation will be to read the instructions, close your eyes, and attempt to do the practice you have just read. But doing involves effort, and effort will keep your mind floating on the surface. So, as you read through this book and practice the techniques, it is important to allow space for nondoing. Sure, you will at first do the practice, but then it is important to relax and let go, and at that point meditation will actually begin. As you progress, nondoing will pervade more and more of your practice. This will become clearer once you get into the actual instruction.

To assist in the process of letting go and allowing space for nondoing, I've broken the instructions for each meditation into simple and easy-to-learn stages. This approach is hardly unique; even traditionally, meditation is typically taught in stages, with the techniques becoming progressively more sophisticated. Likewise, in this book, you will learn stage by stage, but this means reading the book from the beginning, without skipping ahead. Practice each stage of the meditation at your own pace; when you feel comfortable with it, proceed to the next section without any sense of hurry. It may take you only a single sitting to master a given stage, or it may take you a week or more of regular practice. If you spend a week or two at a given stage, that's totally fine. Just move through the book at your own pace. Because of the uniqueness of the practices, you'll get the most out of the book by taking it easy, one step at a time, even if you are an experienced meditator.

Whatever your pace, make a commitment to yourself to finish the book and to meditate regularly while you're learning. Meditate daily, even if only for a few minutes. As you progress through this book, your personal experience will complement your reading. By the end of the book, you will have learned all you need to know to meditate on your own and to receive the benefits of meditation for the rest of your life.

CHAPTER 1

WHAT IS MEDITATION?

Jesus did it. The Buddha did it. Mystics, saints, and sages of spiritual traditions from around the world, and throughout the ages, have spent countless hours doing it. Why has meditation been at the core of the human search for truth and meaning throughout the millennia? Why meditate? What is it?

Albert Einstein once wrote, "The fairest thing we can experience is the mysterious. It is the fundamental emotion which stands at the cradle of true art and true science." It seems that the attraction of meditation has, traditionally at least, been just this: it offers a window into the mystery of our very existence. Meditation is the Hubble Space Telescope for exploring the vast inner space of the soul. Yet here, no external instrument is required; you can meditate on the shores of a holy river, in the comfort of your bedroom, or even in the bus on your way home from work. Only the mind and awareness are needed, nothing else. Meditation is simply the mind turning within to look upon itself.

So what happens when the mind turns within? There are hundreds of forms of meditation, and each may give rise to a variety of experiences. (As we shall see, the inner space of the mind is vast.) Yet all successful forms of meditation have at least one thing in common: sooner or later, *they make the mind's activity subtler*. Put another way, through meditation you transcend your ordinary mental activity to experience quieter and deeper levels of mental activity that are closer to the core of your being.

There are subtle and gross levels to everything. This book in your hands, for instance, appears to be solid and more or less inert matter, but this is only at the gross level of the book's existence. Were you to enter into it more deeply, you would discover that this book is not inert at all. It consists of innumerable molecules shimmering with motion. Were your investigation to go further, you would discover that these pages hold inconceivable power at the subatomic level. Transcending even this level, the subatomic particles that compose this book dissolve into a state of pure potentiality. This pure, abstract potentiality is described by quantum field theory as the vacuum state. This book that you hold in your hands is truly a mystery beyond comprehension. The energy it contains is unimaginable, and on the deepest level of the book's existence it is interrelated with the entire universe.

This is no less true of you and me. We, too, have many levels to our existence. Just as we normally see only the most superficial level of the book, so we ordinarily see only the most superficial level of the body and mind — the gross material body and the conscious thinking mind. Yet just as with the book, the subtler levels hold immense energy and potential, and it is the allure of these deeper levels that has fascinated adepts of meditation throughout the centuries. These deeper levels are much more intimate with our essence and source. Indeed, they hold the very secrets of our existence.

This is why at the heart of all the great spiritual traditions of the world, there are various forms of meditation — spiritual practices that quiet the mind to allow seekers to explore the deeper regions of their being. The mystics of the world's spiritual traditions discovered that as their vision opened to these hidden layers of life, the presence of the Divine became an immediate, vital experience — and they have universally declared that this experience requires no special talent. It is open to any and all who are willing to dedicate themselves to exploring their own inner depths.

Of course, meditation also offers many practical benefits for mental, emotional, and physical health — and because it's a direct experience, it requires no particular religious or spiritual belief. Whether you are interested for spiritual or other reasons — such as to sleep better; to reduce stress, anxiety, and depression; to improve physical health; or to tap your latent creative potential — just regularly meditate as instructed in this book. All that you want lies within you, in the depths of your own being. You need only access it.

THE TWO ESSENTIAL PRINCIPLES OF MEDITATION

Before you set out to explore your inner depths through meditation, it's important to understand a couple of essential principles. These two principles will open the door to actually experiencing the full range of meditation, from the conscious thinking mind to your inmost core. In fact, after these, all else amounts to just the details of particular techniques. They are:

1. Real meditation takes place with sublime ease.
2. Thoughts are a natural feature of meditation.

Essential Principle 1. Sublime Ease

Perhaps you have the impression that meditation is hard to do. It must be for a gifted few with orderly, peaceful minds, right? Nothing could be further from the truth. Meditation can be easy for anyone. In fact, as you'll soon see for yourself, it *has* to be easy or it won't work. That's why the principle of ease is essential to every practice in this book.

Yet this principle appears to contradict common sense: to achieve anything of value in this world requires effort. Just look around. Humankind's greatest achievements — in science and technology, in building corporations, in the creative arts — have been the product of effort. And those who made the effort to discover, build, or create those achievements also made the effort to acquire the knowledge necessary to excel in their fields. When it comes to meditation, however, the only effort required is to make the time to do it. Granted, this can be a challenge in our busy, achievement-oriented society, but once you're actually sitting down and you close your eyes and begin, no effort is required. In fact, effort at that point will land you *further from success*.

Why does effort yield positive results in nearly everything except the process of meditation? Simply put, achievement in the world is in the field of action, in the field of doing; meditation is in the field of being. Meditation is about doing less and less until you are doing nothing, simply being, abiding in the core of your innermost Self. At that point, the ego-mind, which is accustomed to always doing and trying, has temporarily dissolved. This is why meditation is effortless, why it must be effortless: the ego-mind can't dissolve itself by doing. Doing only keeps it intact.

In this respect, meditation is much like falling asleep (another common case of shifting from the waking state to another state of consciousness). Consider what happens every night when you go to bed. You turn off the lights, lie down, and after some time passes, you fall asleep. When it comes, sleep comes effortlessly. Other than setting up the proper conditions for sleep — turning off the lights, lying down comfortably, and so on — you can't *do* falling asleep. In fact, as every insomniac knows, the more you try to fall asleep, the more surely you will lie awake tossing and turning. Only when you completely forget about trying to fall asleep does sleep come.

The same holds true for meditation: making an effort to meditate only interferes with the process. You will have the best meditation when you approach it with the innocence of a child falling asleep. The child is simply tired, and so nature takes over and sleep comes, with ease. As Christ said, the kingdom of heaven is within you, and you must be as innocent as a child to enter it.

Throughout our lives we have all learned to make an effort to one degree or another in order to achieve our goals. This may bring us success in the world, but not peace or fulfillment. For fulfillment, both the inner and outer aspects of life need to be full. We must become as expert in the field of being as we are in the field of doing. This will not only bring inner peace and well-being, but it will also allow us to tap our full creative potential to be even more successful in our active lives.

Essential Principle 2. Thoughts Are Okay

What is the greatest obstacle to meditation? When I ask this question of students in my classes, I usually hear one of two things: "I don't have the time to meditate" or "My mind is just too active to meditate." Notice that both of these relate to being too busy: either my life is too busy or my mind is too busy. In any case, let's consider each of these separately, starting with the time issue.

I empathize with anyone with a busy life. But is a busy schedule really a good reason not to meditate? As Mahatma Gandhi is reported to have said, "I have so much to accomplish today that I must meditate for two hours instead of one." He makes a good point. Just consider how important your mind is to the quality of your life. Your mind is the filter through which you experience everything. The quality of every experience, of every moment of your life, is colored by the quality of your thinking, of your awareness. If you are well rested, relaxed, clear, creative, happy, peaceful, you're going to enjoy your life a whole lot more and achieve a whole lot more. If your productivity and the quality of your entire experience of life can be improved by spending a few minutes a day meditating, isn't that a good investment of time? Meditation pays back that time with megadividends and improves your health and vitality as well. So the fact is, the busier you are, the more important it is to meditate. You just need to put the quality of life, creativity, and productivity at the top of your daily to-do list.

Now, what of the "my mind is too busy to meditate" issue? Everyone's mind is incredibly busy. We all have lots of thoughts; estimates range from thirty thousand to eighty thousand thoughts each day. Whatever the actual number, it's a lot. Yet a busy mind is not an obstacle to meditation. As a wonderful teacher of mine, Mata Amritananda Mayi (Amma, "the hugging saint"), once said, "To say that only those with quiet minds can meditate is like saying that only those with perfect health can go to the doctor." Those with busy minds are the ones who need meditation the most. That's all of us!

Having lots of thoughts does not pose an obstacle to meditation, but the idea that you shouldn't have thoughts in meditation does. In fact, this can be a huge obstacle to meditation. This idea will pit you against your own mind, because it will make you try to suppress your thoughts. That is, you'll break the first essential principle of sublime ease. Besides, the battle against thoughts is a battle you just can't win. The very nature of your mind is to think; that's what a mind does. If you pit yourself against the nature of your mind to think, there will be a loser, and it will be you!

Here is an experiment you can try in order to see this for yourself. See if you can control your mind. Pick something — anything at all — to focus on, and try to focus exclusively on that without any thoughts interrupting your focus for a minute, or even for just fifteen seconds. Seriously, give it a try....

How did you do? Interesting how, the moment you try to focus, other thoughts crowd in. It's almost like magic. The mind's very nature is opposed to control; just like you, your mind wants to be free. So let it. Don't oppose your mind; work with it. That's the Tao of meditation. We don't control the mind, and yet the mind does quiet down. The mind becomes controlled, but not by you or me; rather — and this is a great secret of meditation — the mind can be effortlessly controlled by its own nature.

How can the unruly mind control itself? Well, actually the mind is not so unruly. There is a method to its madness, and that method is this: the mind is spontaneously drawn to greater pleasure, greater happiness. The freedom your mind wants is precisely the freedom you want: to seek your own happiness.

Aren't we all naturally drawn to what we feel will make us happy? This is true whether we seek a satisfying career, a wonderful soul mate, a beautiful home, car, boat, the latest smartphone, our favorite dessert, sex, fame, wealth — whatever we feel might bring us happiness. The mind automatically feels attracted to it. We can't help it. This draw toward greater happiness permeates the mind. In the words of Johann Wolfgang von Goethe, "Happiness is a ball after which we run wherever it rolls, and we push it with our feet when it stops."

I would go so far as to say that this pull toward perceived happiness is to the mind what the law of gravity is to physical objects — it is that powerful a force within us, invisibly driving humanity in all its endeavors. The good news is that when it comes to meditation, this powerful force is not an obstacle. Yes, those who try to control the mind will find its restless search for happiness to be an obstacle. For them the mind will be like a monkey jumping wildly from limb to limb. Yet as my first teacher, Maharishi Mahesh Yogi, used to say, the mind is not a wild monkey at all, but a bumblebee going from flower to flower in search of nectar. Once we understand this, we can simply point the mind in the direction of that nectar of greater happiness instead of trying to forcibly control it. The mind's own nature will begin to work *for* us instead of against us. This is the great secret of effortless meditation.

So, where is greater happiness for the mind? Simply put, it is in transcending to subtler levels of the mind. Once you approach meditation with ease, you will discover the great charm that lies within, in the inner peace, stillness, expansiveness, intelligence, and creativity at the quieter levels of awareness. Once you stop trying to control it, your mind will discover that the experience of its own depths is true nectar. Meditation is said to bring you to what in Sanskrit is called *ananda*, a state of bliss. You don't need to force your mind to go to bliss; you need only point your mind in the right direction and let go, and the law of gravity of the mind — the draw toward greater happiness — will do the rest. This is why the Tao of meditation works best. This is the practical way to control the mind, not by any exertion. You will see just how to do this as we progress through the book. Every technique in this book is based on this principle.

Does this mean you won't have thoughts while meditating? Not at all. As long as you have a mind, you will have thoughts. But once you allow your mind to transcend toward the charm that lies within, the thoughts become less and less significant. Let them come and go; they are not your concern. In this way, you become released from the grip of thoughts; your mind is freed to follow its natural attraction to peace, stillness, expansion, and inner delight. And at times the thoughts will cease, and at that point you will be in the state of "no mind." (More on this later.)

To better understand how thoughts can coincide with deep meditation, allow me to offer a final metaphor. Think of your mind as an ocean. Until now you've been hanging out on the surface of that ocean — the conscious thinking level — bouncing from one thought wave to the next, buffeted by desires, musings, worries, irritations, ambitions, insights, and so on. Once you start to meditate, you slip beneath the surface and begin to descend into the depths of your mind. As soon as you slip beneath the surface, you experience inner silence; and as you descend, the silence becomes deeper, richer, and filled with the light of being. Yet the waves on the surface will likely continue. The whole ocean does not have to become perfectly still for you to experience the inner silence of meditation. You can abide deep within, drawn by that increasing peace and well-being, while thoughts go by on the surface of your mind. And now and then you will rest on the ocean's floor, where all is still....

PURE BEING AND YOUR INMOST SELF

Up to this point I've made several references to the term *being*. I'll continue to refer to it throughout the book as well, because it's something you will experience in meditation. To understand what I mean by *being*, let's consider in more detail what happens in meditation.

I have said that meditation makes the mind's activity subtler. But what does this mean? Essentially, you begin with awareness of the object of meditation at the conscious thinking level. This object could be a mantra, an inner image, your breath, or sensations within your body, to name a few possibilities. Through the process of meditation, you then become aware of that object at a subtler or quieter level of mind, where the boundaries of thought are fainter and more abstract. Then you transcend to still quieter levels, until your awareness of the object is just a faint impulse of consciousness. Then even that faintest impulse may dissolve. At that point you are not asleep — you are still aware — but there is no longer any object of awareness. There is only awareness itself — simple, pure awareness, unrestricted by any boundaries of thought or experience.

In that state of pure awareness, you are no longer doing anything, you are no longer thinking; you are simply being. You are beyond all activity. So I use the word *being* as both a noun and a verb: you are in the state of pure being (noun), and you are simply being (verb). Yet this state of being transcends all things and all actions. It also transcends the mind, which otherwise is constantly engaged in thought. For that reason, pure awareness is sometimes called the state of "no mind."

Much could be said about this state of pure being, but a particularly significant point is this: it is the most interior aspect of you. It is your highest Self. To appreciate this, let's try an exercise. I'd like you to try to intellectually locate the essence of you — that is, attempt to answer the question "Who am I?" Philosophers from both East and West have long asked this question. Plato, for instance, echoed an ancient Greek aphorism when he said, "Know thyself." Why should we do so? Because the answer promises to tell us something important about the meaning of life, at least about the meaning of *our* lives.

Realizing the Self has been the Holy Grail for spiritual seekers in many cultures throughout the millennia. So let's try it.

Let's start this inquiry from the most obvious level, the physical body. It is only natural to strongly identify with your body. For instance, if you have a flu virus, you may say, "I am sick." Yet it is your body that has the virus. Is your body who you really are? Isn't it true that there is something interior to your body that is more essentially "you"? Try to find that inmost essence of you.

For instance, what is a more intimate aspect of you in your experience right now? You may notice, for instance, that your thoughts or feelings are somehow closer to you than your body is. Is that who you are, then, your thoughts and feelings? But your thoughts and feelings come and go. Isn't it true that something else, an even more intimate aspect of you, underlies your thoughts and feelings? What is that?

The sages of the East have for centuries identified that underlying "Self" as simply the awareness in which all thoughts and feelings occur and on which all experience depends. You must be aware to perceive, to think, to feel. Your awareness underlies all these, and all these occur within the "space" of awareness. What could be more interior to you than this abstract inner space of consciousness? Anything else would be an object of awareness.

Awareness, then, is ever the pure subject, the knower, the seer. It is the most intimate aspect of you, your inmost Self. Pure awareness is unrestricted by any boundary of thought or experience, and so your Self is unbounded, infinite. It is beyond form, entirely nonmaterial; your Self is pure Spirit. As the Katha Upanishad attests, "The Self that is subtler than the subtle and greater than the great is lodged in the heart of [every] creature" (1.2.20).

So this is the range of Effortless Mind meditation: from the conscious thinking mind to your inmost, universal Self. However, if this discussion seems abstract to you, or you don't especially care about the spiritual dimension of meditation, you can still meditate and receive all the practical benefits for your body and mind. As my first teacher used to say, if you water the root — the field of pure being, pure awareness — all aspects of the tree of your life will flourish and you will enjoy the fruits.

Now let's prepare for the direct experience of being, with a simple, practical exercise — the yogi's secret advantage — that will help ensure your meditation is effortless and profound.

CHAPTER 2

PREPARING
TO MEDITATE

Meditation is a mental technique, but it involves more than just your mind. For instance, during meditation you will feel your body relax and your breathing become fainter. This shows that your body is intimately involved in the meditation. Not only is your physical body involved, but a subtler level of your body is as well. It is a common experience during meditation to feel filled with energy and/or light; sometimes people report feeling energy flow along the spine or into the head. Such experiences take place at a finer level of your body — at the level of the "energetic body."

THE ENERGETIC BODY

As we saw in chapter 1, there are subtle and gross layers to everything, and this includes your body as well. Even Western science tells us there is a great deal of electrochemical activity in the body, and modern physicists say that all matter is energy. Because we have the gift of this highly sophisticated human nervous system, we are capable of directly experiencing an energetic level of our own being.

Over the centuries, this energetic body has been thoroughly explored by the great researchers of the East: India's yogis, meditating long hours in remote huts and caves. As they describe it, energy flows through a network of innumerable subtle channels throughout the body. They refer to this energy as *prana* (usually translated as "life force") and to the innumerable channels through which the prana flows as *nadis*. The *chakras* (major centers of energy and consciousness in the body), which we will discuss in the next chapter, are another key feature of the energetic body.

In most people, the energetic body operates at a diminished capacity, the flow of subtle energies restricted by impurities. From the yogic perspective, this diminished flow of prana weakens a person's mind and body, restricts consciousness and spiritual experience, and ultimately may result in illness. This concept is hardly unique to India. In China the energetic body has been recognized in terms of chi flowing through subtle channels called meridians, and the balanced and harmonious flow of chi is considered to result in optimal health, while restricted or imbalanced chi is a cause of illness.

What does all this have to do with preparing for meditation? The point is that these three aspects of your being — the physical body, energetic body, and mind — are interrelated. If you do something to one of these, the other two will be affected. This offers a great key to preparing for meditation.

By working on either the energetic body or the physical body in ways conducive to meditation, you can deepen your meditation and accelerate your progress. It will also make meditating much easier. By properly preparing, you will fall into deep meditation without effort.

Practicing yoga postures is one way to work on the physical body to prepare for deeper meditations. People practicing yoga often find that in certain poses they spontaneously experience a meditative state. When properly performed, yoga postures tone the functioning of the nervous system in a way that aids meditation. Working on the energetic body, however, can even more quickly and profoundly prepare you for deep meditation. The energetic body is subtler than the physical body, and as we saw in the previous chapter, the subtle levels of existence are always more powerful than the gross ones. The energetic body is also the connecting point between the physical body and the mind. When you tone the energetic body — by awakening the subtle energies in the body (prana) and getting them to flow in a balanced, harmonious way through the nadis — the physical body's functioning is calmed and revitalized, and the mind is empowered, cleared, and focused.

Here are a few more benefits of toning the energetic body:

- As prana is enlivened and directed to flow through the nadis, obstructions to that flow are dissolved and the chakras, or centers of spiritual energy, become clear and open. This strengthens and normalizes the functioning of the body and mind, releases blocks to creative and healthy expression of the personality, and awakens higher, spiritual consciousness.

- As the obstructions to the flow of prana are dissolved, the prana begins to flow in a more balanced, harmonious way throughout the body. Not only does this improve physical health, but it also improves psychological and emotional health and vitality. When the energetic body is in balance, the physical, mental, and emotional bodies become balanced as well.

- The radiance of the energetic body is the aura that surrounds a person. When the energetic body is constricted by obstructions to the flow of prana, the omnipresent grace of the Divine that is always available to everyone cannot be received. It goes unfelt and unnoticed. When the energetic body is purified — when the obstructions are dissolved — the aura expands and shines brightly and divine grace is experienced and enjoyed. One begins to live a higher expression of life in all ways, spiritually and materially. One walks the earth in the presence of the Divine.

There are many ways to tone the energetic body. Certain breathing practices (*pranayama*) are highly effective in this respect, but these are difficult to teach properly in a book (see the Resources section toward the end of this book). Yet there is one simple exercise that is easily learned and is outstanding for toning the energetic body: *mulabandha*.

MULABANDHA:
THE YOGI'S SECRET ADVANTAGE

In the early 1920s an American physician developed a technique called progressive muscle relaxation, which involves contracting and then relaxing muscle groups. This commonly practiced technique generates a state of relaxation and reduces anxiety. Countless centuries ago, India's yogis discovered a similar practice, but one that in my opinion is more profound. It involves one particular muscle group that when contracted and then relaxed awakens the spiritual energies in the body and directs them upward to stimulate the experience of higher consciousness. While progressive muscle relaxation creates a positive effect primarily in the body and mind, this yogic technique creates a positive effect in the body, in the mind, and most especially in the energetic body. It awakens the prana from the root chakra, located at the perineum, and directs it upward, clearing and opening the primary nadis (those in and around the spine) and the chakras.

The Sanskrit name for this exercise is *mulabandha*. *Mula* means root, and *bandha* means lock. Mulabandha consists of "locking" and then relaxing the muscles at the location of the root chakra, awakening the spiritual energy in that area and directing it upward. Accomplished yogis consider mulabandha to be a master key that unlocks the spiritual energy that is the basis of living in higher consciousness.

For many years, I taught this practice only to advanced students. Then I discovered that when I taught it to those just learning meditation, they began to quickly have the experiences of advanced students. For that reason I made it the foundation of the chakra meditation in Effortless Mind, which you will learn in the next few chapters. Even by practicing it in isolation, you will feel deeply calmed and revitalized.

Posture

To begin the practice, sit comfortably on a cushion or mat with your legs crossed, or sit in a chair with your feet on the floor. The two most important considerations when it comes to position (for this exercise and for all the meditation practices taught in this book) are that you sit comfortably and that you have good posture, with your back and neck comfortably straight.

Some people have the misconception that to meditate really well, you need to sit in a pretzel position. Not true! There are advantages, on an energetic level, to sitting in lotus position or another advanced posture, but these advantages quickly become disadvantages if you are uncomfortable or in pain. Discomfort will only distract you and spoil your meditation.

If you are not used to sitting in the lotus, half-lotus, or other advanced postures, feel free to sit in an ordinary cross-legged position. If your knees don't touch the floor, support them with pillows. Put a pillow under your sacrum to help you sit erect. Or if you prefer, simply sit in a chair with your feet planted on the ground and your spine straight (not slouched). In other words, sit erect but comfortably. In the words of Adi Shankara, renowned Indian philosopher-yogi-saint of the eighth and ninth centuries, the best posture is one "in which the meditation of Brahman flows spontaneously and unceasingly, and not any other [posture] that destroys one's happiness."

It is, however, better to sit than to lie down when meditating, for two reasons:

- If you meditate while lying down, you may fall asleep simply because you are relaxed and in a position ready for sleep.
- When you are seated with good posture, the energies are drawn upward to awaken the higher energy centers. When you're lying down, the energies are not so naturally drawn upward.

That said, if you have a physical disability or are in pain while sitting and need to lie down while meditating, by all means do lie down. You will still receive great benefit from meditation.

As for placement of your hands, comfort is, again, the important thing. At this point, you needn't be overly concerned with any particular position of the hands. You can simply rest your hands easily on your lap or on your knees. There are many traditional positions for hand placement during meditation, called *mudras*, which I discuss in chapter 8.

Practice

Begin by closing your eyes and breathing just a little deeper than normal through your nose, inhaling and exhaling at a steady, relaxed pace. Notice the flow of breath in and out of your nostrils. Let your breaths become long and quiet. Feel your whole body relaxing. After a minute or so of this, as you breathe in, firmly but without strain contract the perineum (the muscles between the anus and genitals, where the root chakra is located).

At the end of your in-breath, hold the breath and the contraction of the muscles of the perineum momentarily. As you breathe out, relax the perineum completely. As you practice, see if you can isolate the muscles of the perineum without any strain, so that only this area contracts. Continue for a couple of minutes in this way. When you have finished, continue to sit with your eyes closed and just be. Enjoy any sense of inner silence or peace. Note how you feel in body and mind. Very likely even two minutes of this practice will result in an increased sense of peace and alertness.

When you're ready, try it again. This time, as you breathe in, squeeze your perineum and gently feel your attention flow up the spine from your perineum to the crown of your head. As you breathe out and relax your perineum, gently feel your attention descend from the crown of your head back down the spine to your perineum. Do not make any effort to visualize or try to have any particular experience. Just allow a gentle, easy, abstract flow of attention with no expectations — up the spine with the in-breath as you squeeze the perineum, and down the spine with the out-breath as you relax the perineum.

Perhaps your attention does not seem restricted to your spine, or perhaps the flow of attention seems unclear. This is okay. Just be easy with it. Ease allows your awareness to move to subtler levels of experience; and again, the subtle is more powerful. Adding this faint flow of attention up and down the spine will significantly deepen your sense of inner silence and peace. After a couple of minutes, stop and simply be. Enjoy whatever peace and stillness you feel.

This gentle yogic practice is one of many similar exercises practiced by India's yogis for centuries. Practice it easily and gently until you feel comfortable and familiar with it. This does not mean that you need to feel the flow of attention clearly; it is likely to remain a faint, abstract flow. When you do feel at ease with the practice, then you're ready to combine mulabandha with chakra meditation to bring far greater results.

CHAPTER 3

CHAKRA MEDITATION

Chakra meditation is a wonderful ancient practice that makes deep meditation immediately accessible. It is the meditation practice I teach first because it awakens the subtle energies and begins to clear the energetic body, so that everything that follows will be greatly enhanced.

SETTING YOUR INTENTION

Before starting to actually meditate, it is important to set your intention for the meditation. I'm not speaking here of deciding what benefits you will gain from your meditation. For the most part, the benefits of meditation will come spontaneously, though you certainly may set the intention that your meditation will yield particular benefits or support a particular outcome. Here, however, I'm referring to setting an intention that the meditation will benefit not only you but others as well.

This is an important principle. Naturally you meditate for the benefits you will gain, and it's entirely healthy to allot this time each day for the sake of your well-being. But if you are meditating only with the thought of your own benefit, albeit your own betterment, then to some slight degree meditation may become a selfish act. Selfishness does not serve the deeper spiritual purpose of meditation, which is to make us more compassionate, caring, generous, and selfless. Almost miraculously, however, we can turn this potential selfishness inside out by simply having the sincere intention that others will benefit by our practice.

Meditating for others? Yes, we can and do influence the world by our meditation — in fact, by everything we do. On the most obvious level, you can positively or negatively influence each and every person you meet without even being aware of it. A sour disposition can spread frustration and stress to others; a bright disposition can uplift. You can ruin someone's day or you can make someone's day, and not just that of one person but of many. Think of all the people you connect with in a given day.

You may not ordinarily be aware of it, but you influence your surroundings at invisible and powerful levels as well. At the gross level of your being (your physical body), you may seem to end at your skin. At subtler levels, however, your influence extends beyond your body. We've already spoken of the energetic body and the aura, which is the radiance of your energetic body. Your aura extends well beyond the boundaries of your physical body; it may even extend many yards in all directions around you, subtly influencing everyone and everything within your energetic field.

Have you ever encountered a violent person? His or her mere presence will make you uneasy. If you encounter someone who is extraordinarily clear, loving, and joyful, you will feel that too. You will feel at ease and uplifted in his or her presence and, as a result, be attracted to that person. When your energetic body is clear and your prana flows harmoniously, the vibrational influence you emanate raises the joy, happiness, peace, and clarity in all those around you.

Entering meditation with the intention to uplift and benefit all beings aligns your individual ego-mind with this possibility of uplifting others, and so expands the meaning of meditation for you. Having this intention to be selfless every time you meditate also erodes selfishness. So begin your meditation by setting your intention to bring the highest good to the universe and to all beings. You may use your own words, but here is a suggestion: "May the merit and benefits of this meditation be multiplied infinitely to bring peace and happiness to all beings."

Another aspect of your intention as you begin your meditation may be gratitude for the sacredness of the process. You are about to dive into your inner depths, to commune with your higher Self, the Divine within you. It is a sacred process and a great gift. You may reflect for a moment to appreciate the sacred gift of meditation as you begin your practice.

THE CHAKRA SYSTEM

An important aspect of the energetic body is the chakra system. Chakras are centers of energy and consciousness in the body. Descriptions of such centers, particularly along the spine and in the head, have been found in spiritual traditions in many parts of the world. They are found in the Vedic, Yogic, and Tantric traditions of India, in Tibetan Buddhism, in Sufism, and even in Mayan spirituality. Related descriptions of spiritual energy in the body and subtle pathways conducting that energy (*nadis* in Sanskrit) are found in ancient Goddess cultures of Europe, traditional Chinese medicine, and ancient Egyptian texts. Even the accounts of Christian mystics like Saint Teresa of Avila bear remarkable resemblance to experiences related to the opening of the chakras and spiritual energy described by Indian yogis. Such experiences have arisen in so many divergent cultures for one reason: spiritual energy and the chakras are not simply concepts; they are real and open to investigation and experience by anyone.

My first personal experience of the chakras took place in the early 1970s, before I had so much as given a thought to the chakras. In fact, it happened while I was in a light sleep. I was on an extended retreat, practicing for many hours a day a form of meditation that had nothing to do with chakras in any overt sense. On this particular day I'd had several especially deep meditations. That night, shortly after I fell asleep, I felt a surge of spiritual power seemingly drawn from my inner thighs into my perineum, where I experienced an intense ball of energy and light. That power was drawn up through my body, and as it reached the location of each chakra, it flared into a bright ball of energy, one chakra after another in quick succession. When it entered my head, the brilliant light brought me to full awareness and I woke up.

For me, this unexpected and unsolicited experience of the

chakras was proof of their existence. Not only had I not yet studied the chakras and knew nothing about them, but also I was asleep during the experience. It took place without any anticipation, yet was entirely vivid. The energy had been real. I had no sense whatsoever that I had been merely dreaming. Since that day long ago, I've experienced the chakras countless times in meditation, further validating (for me at least) their existence. Of course this may not convince anyone else of the existence of the chakras, but that doesn't matter. Believing in chakras is not the point. The point is to experience and open them.

First, a few basics about the chakras. The word *chakra* literally means "circle" or "wheel." There are many such centers of energy and consciousness throughout the body, seven of which are identified as primary ones.

The first five of these are associated with elements; for instance, the root chakra is associated with the earth element. This is not an arbitrary association; the chakra is actually the locus in the body for that element. Clearing the chakra strengthens, balances, and harmonizes the particular element in the body, resulting in benefits to the mind, body, and personality.

The following is a description of the location of each of the primary chakras and a brief summary of the benefits of opening each one. We'll examine these benefits in more detail in chapter 10.

1. MULADHARA, OR THE ROOT CHAKRA (EARTH ELEMENT).
   The root chakra is located in the area of the perineum

between the anus and genitals. Clearing and opening the root chakra releases negative and contracting instincts relating to security and survival. As a result of this clearing and opening, you feel trusting in life, safe and secure, happy, with a sense of self that is solid and grounded.

2. SVADHISHTHANA, OR THE SACRAL CHAKRA (WATER ELEMENT). The sacral chakra is located at the base of the spine near the tip of the tailbone. Clearing and opening the sacral chakra releases attachments, addictions, and tendencies to repress desires and emotions. The result is a harmonious relationship with your emotions and sexuality and ease of creative expression. Like a pure, unimpeded stream, you flow with your natural emotions and desires, and with your life as a whole.

3. MANIPURA, OR THE NAVEL CHAKRA (FIRE ELEMENT). The navel chakra is located in the spine at the level of the navel. Clearing and opening the navel chakra releases issues relating to personal power, including anxieties and fears or a need to dominate. The result is a genuine, expansive, secure sense of personal power characterized by acceptance and tolerance of others. When you have cleared the navel chakra, you will attract others and be a natural leader. Your personal power will shine in a balanced way that benefits yourself and others.

4. ANAHATA, OR THE HEART CHAKRA (AIR ELEMENT). The heart chakra is located in the spine at the level of the

heart. Clearing and opening the heart chakra releases emotional attachments and selfishness, resulting in unconditional love, compassion, well-being, and devotion. Like the air shared by all beings, your love nourishes all.

5. VISHUDDHA, OR THE THROAT CHAKRA (SPACE ELEMENT). The throat chakra is located in the spine at the level of the base of the throat. Clearing and opening the throat chakra releases issues relating to an inability to find and speak your truth. This results in authentic and eloquent self-expression. You naturally abide in your higher Self, and your speech expresses the truth of your whole being.

6. AJNA, OR THE THIRD-EYE CHAKRA (MIND). This chakra is located in the center of the head at the level of the eyebrows. Clearing and opening the ajna chakra releases the tendency to cling to a gross material perception of life or an overreliance on dry rationality and rejection of the spiritual and intuitive. The result is genuine spiritual vision and intuition — a clear, deep perception of the inner reality of life. This is the opening of the eye of wisdom.

7. SAHASRARA, OR THE CROWN CENTER (TRANSCENDENTAL PURE CONSCIOUSNESS). The crown center is located at the crown of the head. Clearing and opening this center unties the knot of identification with ego and separation from others, resulting in an expansive and blissful realization of the Infinite, of oneness with all, enlightenment.

Note that although it is good to have some understanding of the chakras, when it comes to actually meditating, all you need to know is the location of the chakras. Beyond that, simply enjoy the innocent experience, free of ideas. That is the best way to ensure you get the full benefits of the meditation.

STEPS OF THE MEDITATION

Once you are comfortable that you know the location of the chakras, read the following steps a couple of times, as well as the section that follows, "Ending the Meditation." When you clearly understand the steps, close your eyes and practice. You may need to peek at the instructions at first. This is fine. After a couple of sessions, you won't need to.

Most importantly, as you perform each step in the process, *relax and let go*. Be receptive, but without an expectation of any particular experience. Give the process space to occur naturally. It is not your effort or expectation that accomplishes the meditation; in fact, these will only get in the way. Rather, by letting go and remaining receptive, you allow the "force of gravity" inherent in the mind, the attraction to inner bliss, to take you within. This is when meditation really begins.

Like everyone, you will inevitably have thoughts while you meditate. Recall that this is part of the meditation and does not interfere with it at all. It's perfectly fine to have thoughts in meditation, even plenty of them. Simply pay no attention to them. Let them go as they come, like clouds floating by in the sky above. They can be there, but you don't have to show an interest in them. During most of your life, you have given much attention to your thoughts — even feeding them with your attention — but in meditation you can adopt an attitude of dispassion toward them. Don't feed them, but don't try to push them away either. When you notice that you have become engaged in thoughts, easily return to the steps of the meditation.

Finally, during meditation you enter into delicate realms of experience, which are inherently faint and abstract. Do not try to feel or experience anything clearly. Effort to do so will only agitate the mind and bring you to a more superficial experience. Have no expectations. Perhaps, for instance, you don't feel any energy, or perhaps you feel the chakras in the core of your body or near the front of your body instead of in the spine. That's fine. Just be open to experiencing everything as it comes. If you don't feel anything, don't worry about it. Clarity of inner perception will develop over time. For now, just enjoy your experience — whatever it may be.

Here are the steps of the first stage of chakra meditation:

1. Sit comfortably with good posture as discussed in chapter 2 in the "Posture" section. Set your intention: "May the merit and benefits of this meditation be multiplied infinitely to bring peace and happiness to all beings." Close your eyes and feel this intention for a few moments. Allow yourself to feel gratitude for the sacred gift of meditation you are about to enjoy.

2. With your eyes closed, breathe naturally through your nose. Gently bring your attention to the area of the root chakra, at the perineum.

3. For three or four breaths, practice mulabandha with your breathing, firmly contracting the perineum with each inhalation and releasing it with each exhalation. As you exhale, feel a sense of warmth or expansion at the root chakra. This is just a faint feeling. Your experience of the chakra does not need to be, nor is it likely to be, crystal clear. (This is true for all the chakras.)

4. Cease mulabandha and relax completely. Simply allow your awareness to sink deeply into the area of the root chakra (perineum), savoring whatever sense of inner

silence you feel there for ten to twenty seconds. This effortless but steady attention, steeped in deep silence, will begin to open the root chakra and activate the energy there. Don't be in a hurry. Simply be and enjoy the silence at the chakra.

5. Again perform mulabandha with your breathing for three or four breaths. As you inhale and squeeze the perineum, draw your awareness into the base of the spine at your tailbone (the site of your sacral chakra). As you exhale and relax the perineum, feel a sense of expansion at your tailbone.

6. Cease mulabandha and just be, letting your awareness rest in inner silence at the sacral chakra. Allow that silence to penetrate more and more deeply into the chakra for ten to twenty seconds.

7. Next move your awareness up to the navel chakra, in the spine at the level of the navel, in the same way. With each inhalation and mulabandha combination, draw the attention up from the root chakra at the perineum into the navel chakra. As you exhale, feel a sense of expansion in the navel chakra.

8. Cease mulabandha and let your awareness rest in inner silence at the navel chakra. Allow that silence to penetrate more and more deeply into the chakra for ten to twenty seconds.

9. After the navel chakra, move in the same way up to the heart chakra, in the spine at the level of the heart. Repeat the practice for this chakra as for the previous chakras.

10. After the heart chakra, move up to the throat chakra, in the spine at the level of the base of the throat. Again repeat the practice.

11. Next, move up to the third-eye chakra, at the point between the eyebrows, and repeat the practice there.

12. Finally, move up to the crown center. In the crown center, after you've stopped mulabandha, allow your mind to completely merge with the deep silence you experience, and sit in that inner silence for twenty seconds to a minute, or even longer, until you feel it's time to come out of meditation. If you have time and you wish to continue meditating, you can bring your attention back to the root chakra, at the perineum, and go through the chakras again.

Here are a few additional points to be aware of as you perform the preceding steps:

• As you draw your attention up from the root chakra to the higher chakras, your inhalations will likely be a little deeper than usual. This is simply because your inhalations are associated with pulling your attention and energy up, and there is a greater distance from the root chakra to the higher chakras. Still, there is no need to exaggerate this with very deep breaths. Gentle, quiet breaths are preferable because the breath and mind are closely related: the more active the breath, the more active the mind; the quieter the breath, the quieter the mind. In other words, you will have a deeper experience if your breath is subtle. As you inhale while moving your attention to the higher chakras, the breath can be somewhat longer and still be quiet and subtle.

- As you draw your attention up from the root chakra to the higher chakras, you may feel your attention flowing up the spine. If it takes another route instead — for instance, up the core of your body — that is perfectly okay. Again, the experience is on a faint level of feeling and so is indistinct. It's unlikely you will feel the flow of your attention consistently restricted to your spine. Simply have the intention to draw your awareness up the spine; whatever you experience as a result is fine.

- As you draw your attention up from the root chakra to the higher chakras, you need not feel the intervening chakras on the way. For instance, as you draw your attention from the root chakra to the heart chakra, you do not have to feel the sacral and navel chakras.

- As you exhale and enjoy the inner silence at a chakra, you may feel the warmth, expansion, or sensations in the spine, in your core, or toward the front of your body. All of these are fine. Although the sacral, navel, heart, and throat chakras are located in the spine, sensations at these chakras are often felt in the core or front of the body (rather than in the spine) because of the energy flowing in the nadis related to the chakras.

ENDING THE MEDITATION

You have just traversed the full range of your being and are in a deep state. Notice how slight your breath is. You may feel you are hardly breathing. If you come out of meditation too quickly, you may jar your body and mind and possibly spoil some of the effects of the meditation. You may even get a headache or feel rough around the edges if you come out too quickly. For these reasons, it is essential to have a smooth transition from the meditative state to your active waking state. Ideally, lie down in the yoga pose called *shavasana*, or "corpse pose." Lie on your back, feet apart about shoulder width, arms relaxed by your sides, palms up and slightly away from your body. Lie like this for three to five minutes, or longer if you like. If you doze off, no problem; just enjoy the relaxation.

If you are meditating where you can't lie down, come out of meditation while sitting; simply stay seated, with eyes closed, for three to five minutes. When coming out in a seated position, you may tend to be drawn back into a meditative state. To transition smoothly to the waking state, very gently rub your fingers a bit. This will draw your attention outward.

Whether coming out in a prone or sitting position, just before you open your eyes and get up, close your meditation with a conscious and specific expression of gratitude. This sets you up to move through your day with heightened awareness and an attitude that will encourage you to naturally give. It will help you to carry the benefits of your meditation forward into the day. You may thank the Divine or higher power for anything in your life that you feel grateful for: for the experience of meditation you've just had, for your spouse or partner, your family, your health, and so on. You will develop your gratitude by expressing thanks for even the most basic things you've been given: for the air you breathe, the clean water you drink, the food you eat; and for your conveniences, such as your car, house, clothes, and so on. No matter what your situation, everyone has something to be grateful for. Living with an attitude of gratitude is key to bringing the grace of meditation into your whole day.

With this closing intention, you may also ask to be an instrument during your day for peace and healing in the hands of the universe or God. Having a heightened awareness of how much you are given, you will find it is only natural to wish to give in return. Yet rather than do so from the limited ego, better to be a channel through which grace can flow from the same source that nurtures you. Feel free to use your own words, but here is a suggestion you might find useful: "Thank you for this life, my wife [or husband], my family, this beautiful earth, my work in the world [and so on — name whatever you feel grateful for]. May I be an instrument of healing and peace in your hands."

Now you are calmed, deepened, and energized — ready to open your eyes and dynamically engage in your day.

Practice this meditation until you are completely comfortable with it. When it becomes easy and you move from one chakra to the next nearly automatically, you're ready for stage 2 of chakra meditation, the incorporation of mantras into the chakra meditation for a deeper and richer experience.

CHAPTER 4

CHAKRA MANTRA
MEDITATION

In the beginning was the Word:
The Word was with God
And the Word was God.

— John 1:1

In the first stage of chakra meditation, you integrated an awareness of the chakras with the practice of mulabandha. In the process, whether you realized it or not, you began to awaken and direct prana through the nadis in and around your spine. You may or may not have felt prana moving in your body (either way is entirely okay), but you probably felt at least some of the effects: a degree of inner stillness and a pleasant sense of peacefulness. This is an excellent beginning, but now we can take this deeper by adding the use of mantras into your practice.

Recall that in chapter 1 we defined meditation as the process of making the mind's activity subtler. Notice that in the first stage of chakra meditation, your breathing became finer and you felt some relaxation and peace; perhaps your mind also became quieter at points. These are all signs that to some extent you transcended to those subtler levels. Yet, to take the mind even deeper, something more is needed. Some medium of experience, some particular thought is needed to provide the mind with a vehicle for transcending through all its subtle layers. If you can give your mind such a vehicle, then it can first experience that thought at a conscious level, then at a subtler level, then a deeper level, until your mind transcends even the faintest level of that thought. The silence that you will then experience will be deeper and richer than the silence you felt during the first stage of chakra meditation.

· One such vehicle for transcendence is called a mantra. A mantra is a syllable, word, or group of words with a very pure and harmonious vibratory quality; chanting it or, even better, silently meditating on it uplifts and purifies your consciousness. Mantras reveal that language is more than simply a means to communicate: language is sound, and sound is vibration, and vibration can have a powerful impact on us.

Modern physics reveals that all matter is vibrating energy. Vibration is an essential aspect of all existence; it determines the qualities, form, and structure of everything. Put another way, vibration (the Word) is the structuring intelligence of everything. India's ancient seers realized this truth through their deep meditations. They saw that vibration structures even the quality of an individual's personality and consciousness, and that affecting vibration was therefore a key to transformation. They further cognized a number of extremely pure and powerful impulses or vibrations within their consciousness. These particular vibrations are the traditional mantras, and they serve as an ideal medium for meditation, for transformation.

From this discussion you can see that mantras are not just words; really, they are vibrations. A word we speak with our mouths that we may call a mantra, like *Om*, for instance, is just the outer package that delivers the actual mantra, which is the essence of the word, its vibratory quality. In fact, you truly experience the mantra (the vibration) only when, during meditation, you transcend the word. This reveals the key to mantra meditation: You start at the conscious, thinking level, mentally thinking the mantra. (There is no need to say it aloud, because you want to go to subtler levels, not bring it out to the gross vocalized level.) At this point, you are thinking a word; you are not yet consciously experiencing the true mantra, which is latent within the word. Then, as you continue to think it, the word gradually fades and becomes just a faint idea, feeling, or impulse. In other words, you are transcending to a subtler experience of the mantra. You are getting into the essence of the mantra, which transcends the word and is vibration.

As you gain greater clarity at these quieter levels of the mind, you may experience the mantra as a steady, pure tone, like a bell ringing through every cell of your being. The Dhyana-Bindu Upanishad describes this: "That man is the knower of the Vedas [divine knowledge] who knows that the end of Pranava [Om] should be worshipped (or recited) as uninterrupted as the flow of oil and (resounding) as long as the sound of a bell."

To continue this analogy presented by the Upanishad, thinking the mantra as a word is like striking a bell; thinking the mantra as a faint idea is like striking the bell more softly; letting go of even the faint idea and experiencing the mantra as a faint feeling, subtle tone, or quality of inner silence is like hearing only the pure tone of the bell as it resonates after being struck. Striking the bell requires some effort; striking it softly requires less; enjoying the tone of the bell requires no effort. In the case of the mantra, however, the vibration does not diminish over time as it does in the case of the bell. The mind savors the feeling (vibration) of the mantra on and on, drinking it in, which elevates the state of one's mind and body, bringing more energy, peace, joy, creativity, love, and expansion.

Again, the subtler levels of the mantra hold much more transformative power than the gross level of word does. This may be compared to homeopathy, which greatly dilutes substances to activate the vital energy and so the healing potency of the substance. A visible amount of the substance — say, a teaspoon of sulfur — may have little effect, whereas the activated homeopathic dilution, with but a few molecules of sulfur, has much more healing potency. The principle behind this is exactly what we discussed in chapter 1 — the subtle levels of existence are always more powerful than the gross. Likewise, the gross, audible word that is the mantra has only a little power to transform, compared to the "diluted" vibration, the essence of the mantra, which holds far more potency.

Sometimes, even after this explanation, people may feel compelled to mentally repeat the mantras clearly, so before starting the meditation, let's try an experiment to help you better understand the importance of thinking the mantra gently. Sit with your eyes closed and notice your thoughts for about half a minute; then open your eyes. Go ahead, try it....

Your thoughts are very abstract, aren't they? They are not a clear pronunciation of words, but faint wisps, hardly recognizable as words at all — and this is how we experience language at the conscious thinking level, which is the grossest level of thought. Meditation is supposed to take us to much more abstract levels of thought. So, if we try to think the mantra as a clear pronunciation, we are actually going in the wrong direction. We are going to a level of thought that is even grosser than the ordinary conscious level of thinking. This means that for the meditation to work, we *must* let go of the clear pronunciation of the mantra. We must allow it to become a faint idea or just a feeling or tone.

So if ever you find yourself hammering away at the mantra clearly, just stop. Sit for a minute without making any attempt to meditate. Just be. When you feel at ease, then gently begin the mantra again, and don't mind a bit if it fades or you feel you are losing the mantra. Let the mental pronunciation of the mantra go and enjoy the faint feeling that follows. That subtle feeling, which may be quite indistinct, is the vibration of the mantra. It is the mantra's essence.

One last point on this: The tendency to think the mantra clearly usually comes from anxiety about correctly pronouncing the mantra. But remember how faint your ordinary thoughts were when you witnessed them a minute ago? They were faint wisps; but if you were to speak your thoughts, they would emerge from your mouth as clearly pronounced words. This means that even though our thoughts are indistinct mental currents, the correct pronunciation of the words is still present in our thoughts; we just don't experience that pronunciation clearly at the mental level. Likewise, once you know the correct pronunciation of a mantra, though it may seem indistinct when you think it, the correct pronunciation is intact. You need not think the mantra clearly or worry that the pronunciation is wrong. You don't need to worry about anything. It is only natural that as the mantra goes to finer and finer levels, your experience of it will change: it will fade or become just a faint impulse, feeling, or tone. This is the experience of the subtle levels of the mantra.

Now, what mantras will we use for our meditation? During Effortless Mind meditation we use a number of mantras for specific purposes. During the chakra meditation, we use what are called seed syllables, one-syllable mantras that are the vibration of the particular element (earth, water, fire, air, or space) associated with each chakra. The element and its mantra relate to the vibratory quality of the chakra. The following table shows the mantra and element associated with each chakra. As for pronunciation of the mantras: the *a* is short, pronounced like the *u* in the word *but*, so the first five mantras all rhyme with *hum*.

CHAKRA	ELEMENT	MANTRA AND PRONUNCIATION
Root (*muladhara*)	Earth	Lam (*Lum*)
Sacral (*svadhishthana*)	Water	Vam (*Vum*)
Navel (*manipura*)	Fire	Ram (*Rum*)
Heart (*anahata*)	Air	Yam (*Yum*)
Throat (*vishuddha*)	Space	Ham (*Hum*)
Third-eye (*ajna*)	Mind	Om (*Om*)
Crown (*sahasrara*)	Pure consciousness, transcending the universe (beyond all elements)	Transcendent silence

Before you begin this meditation, let me offer another word on the benefits of adding mantras to the chakra meditation. It is one thing to experience silence at the chakras, as in the first stage of chakra meditation, but bringing in vibration has a number of additional advantages:

- Again, using a mantra provides a means for you to transcend to subtler, more powerful layers of consciousness. Without a mantra, you might sit in relative silence at a fairly superficial level of mind. This is not nearly as powerful as the silence you access by transcending to subtle layers of the mind via the mantra.

- Applying the high vibration of the mantras to the area of the chakra accelerates the purification and opening of the chakra. You are essentially using a high, natural vibration to clear and open your chakras, which to some extent are clogged by impurities that have accumulated from past experience. (We'll talk more about such impurities in chapter 9.)

- Because each mantra is the vibration of a particular element related to a particular chakra, applying the vibration of an element at its seat in the body strengthens and balances that element throughout the body, improving health.

- Adding the dimension of sound involves and activates another area of your brain — that area related to the sense of hearing. Engaging more of the brain creates a more holistic awareness, making your meditation more powerful.

STEPS OF THE MEDITATION

The second stage of chakra meditation differs from the first only in the addition of a mantra at each chakra. Here are the steps. Read them all the way through, and do your best to memorize the mantra for each chakra. Then close your eyes and practice. Leave the book open to the preceding table in case you need to take a peek to check a mantra. Initially this might detract somewhat from the meditation, but soon you won't need to peek.

1. Sit comfortably and set your intention: "May the merit and benefits of this meditation be multiplied infinitely to bring peace and happiness to all beings." Close your eyes and feel this intention for a few moments, allowing yourself to feel gratitude for the sacred gift of meditation you are about to enjoy.

2. Breathe naturally through the nose. Close your eyes and gently bring your attention to the area of the root chakra, at the perineum. Now, for three or four breaths, practice mulabandha with your breath, firmly contracting the perineum as you inhale and relaxing it as you exhale. With each exhalation, feel an expansion at the root chakra, and very gently think "Lam" (pronounced *Lum*). Feel the mantra in the area of the chakra as a faint idea or feeling, not as a clear mental pronunciation; the fainter the mantra, the better.

3. Cease mulabandha and continue to gently, easily think "Lam" a few more times at the root chakra. Let the mantra gradually fade into a faint feeling, steady tone,

or silence (any of these is fine). This fading of the mantra will probably happen within a few mental repetitions. If the mantra doesn't fade away on its own after five or six gentle mental repetitions, just consciously let it go and enjoy the feeling or silence that follows. That feeling or silence will be permeated with the resonance of the mantra created by the repetitions. You may also experience a sense of unboundedness. Just be, savoring the feeling or silence or unboundedness at the chakra for ten to twenty seconds.

4. Then, for three or four breaths, perform mulabandha as you inhale, and draw your awareness into the base of the spine at your tailbone (the site of your sacral chakra). As you exhale, feel a sense of expansion at your tailbone and very gently think "Vam" (pronounced *Vum*). Feel the mantra in the sacral chakra.

5. Cease mulabandha and continue to gently, easily think "Vam" a few more times at the sacral chakra. Let the mantra gradually dissolve into a faint feeling, a steady tone, or silence. If the mantra doesn't fade away on its own after five or six gentle mental repetitions, just consciously let it go and enjoy the feeling or silence that follows. Again, you may also experience a sense of unboundedness. Just be, and enjoy the feeling or silence or unboundedness at the sacral chakra for ten to twenty seconds before moving to the next chakra.

6. Now repeat this same procedure for each chakra in turn. At the navel chakra, use the mantra Ram (pronounced *Rum*).

7. At the heart chakra, use Yam (pronounced *Yum*).

8. At the throat chakra, use Ham (pronounced *Hum*).

9. At the third-eye chakra, use Om (pronounced *Om*).

10. At the crown center, allow your awareness to be first absorbed in transcendent silence at the crown of the head, and then feel there an orb of clear light, like the sun or a transcendent full moon. Let your awareness be absorbed in the light. Sit in that absorbed state for a minute or more. (If you don't experience any light, allow your awareness to be absorbed in whatever inner silence and unboundedness you feel at your crown.) Then gently be aware of and feel the subtle light and blissful energy that is now permeating your body.

11. If you have time and you wish to continue meditating, you can bring your attention back to the root chakra at the perineum and go through the chakras again. If you do so, try it without mulabandha this time. Why without mulabandha now? Because it's already done its job. Though mulabandha is a powerful practice, once it has plunged you deep into meditation, you may go even deeper by setting it aside and following your bliss. Let the mantra fade to just a faint feeling or tone at each chakra. Savor that feeling.

12. End the meditation by lying down in the corpse pose for three to five minutes to come out slowly.

13. Finally, before you get up, close your meditation with an expression of gratitude and set an intention for the day to be an instrument in the hands of the Divine: "Thank you for this life, my wife [or husband], my family, this beautiful earth, my job [and so on — name

whatever you feel grateful for]. May I be an instrument of healing and peace in your hands."

Congratulations. You have completed chakra mantra meditation. Continue to practice chakra mantra meditation until you are completely comfortable with it. When you move through the meditation almost automatically, without having to think about what to do next or having to try to recall the mantras, you're ready to move on to the next stage, which will incorporate light to further deepen your experience.

CHAPTER 5

CHAKRA MEDITATION WITH DIVINE LIGHT

In the world's spiritual traditions, light is a common metaphor for spirit, truth, goodness, or the Divine. Christ said:

> *I am the light of the world;*
> *anyone who follows me will not be walking in the dark;*
> *he will have the light of life.*

In India's most revered scripture, the Bhagavad Gita, Krishna, too, describes himself in terms of light:

> *The light that lives in the sun,*
> *Lighting all the world,*
> *The light of the moon,*
> *The light that is in fire:*
> *Know that light to be mine.*

Tibetan Buddhism speaks of the essence of mind as light: "The Clear Light, in its primal aspect, symbolizes the unconditioned, pure *Nirvanic* Consciousness....As being colourless, or without qualities, It is the Clear Light; as being without limitations, It is All-Pervading Intelligence; as being unknowable in terms of sangsaric consciousness, and without form, It is the Formless Void."

The description of the Divine as light in these and other spiritual traditions for so many centuries expresses a universal truth that has been directly experienced by countless mystics throughout the ages: Spirit is light. The Divine is light and your innermost essence is the light of pure awareness, the light that is pure Spirit. You, too, can experience this spiritual light, for it is nothing apart from you. It is the light of your highest Self. Experiencing the light of pure consciousness is another key to transformation, and in the third stage of chakra meditation, you will experience this directly for yourself.

Introducing light into the meditation increases the purifying power of the meditation. Not only is the light itself purifying, but bringing in light activates another portion of the brain — that area of the brain relating to the sense of sight. By engaging more of your brain, you generate a more holistic awareness, enhance the power of your meditation, and accelerate your growth through meditation.

This does raise a question, however: What if you don't see any light? The short answer to this is: no problem. You may or may not perceive light. Simply be open to the possibility. If you don't perceive light, enjoy the subtle experience of the mantra or the silence at the chakra. Eventually, light will come of its own accord as your inner perception develops.

The light of consciousness is extremely subtle, and as in all deep inner experiences, clarity will come in time as you become used to functioning at those delicate layers, and as you are purified in mind and body through regular practice of meditation. Since birth, your attention has been primarily directed outward, engaged through the senses with the material world. This outward focus on the world is entirely natural. Nonetheless, dealing day after day in the material world hardly prepares you to operate in the subtle interior realms of consciousness.

As we saw in chapter 1, there is nothing finer than consciousness. Consciousness is said to be subtler than the subtlest. It allows us to experience everything, and yet it is not experienced. To see this for yourself, try an experiment. You can do this either standing or sitting, with eyes open: For a minute or so, simply see if you can be aware of your own awareness. Try to be aware of your consciousness — that is, the space within which all thought, feeling, and perception occurs, but which is none of these, and which in its character has nothing to do with any of these. See if you can isolate pure awareness itself....

How'd you do? Awareness is pretty abstract, isn't it? Because it's entirely abstract — it has no edges, no boundaries whatsoever — it is not an object at all. It is ever the pure subject. Every feeling you have, every thought you have, every perception is an object of your awareness. Even your personality is an object of which you may be aware. The innermost essence of you is simply beyond anything you can point to or identify as a thing. It is pure, limitless Spirit.

From this, you can see that it stands to reason that going

from a lifetime habit of experiencing the gross material world to experiencing the light of consciousness may take some time, and so patience is needed. There is, however, one secret that may help you to advance more quickly, and it is something you were probably proficient in as a child: imagination.

THE ROLE OF IMAGINATION IN MEDITATION

You may be tempted to think of imagination as the resource of artists and a faculty of childhood, which was a time when most of us exercised the creativity of the mind to explore and play in worlds that were a mix of make-believe and reality. However, imagination — the capacity to internally experience sensations and images that are not "objectively real" — is not for children and artists alone. It plays an important role for all of us, even as adults. Every time we read a book, for instance, we form mental impressions of what we read that allow us to experience what we might not have otherwise experienced, to know things that we might not have otherwise known. Albert Einstein largely attributed his greatest scientific insights not to his considerable scientific understanding but to imagination. As he put it, "Imagination is more important than knowledge. For knowledge is limited, whereas imagination embraces the entire world, stimulating progress, giving birth to evolution." Imagination is not just child's play; it plays a critical role in learning about our world, about life.

Millennia ago, India's yogis discovered the value of imagination. Like Einstein, they found that imagination — especially when developed and refined through deep meditation

— opens the door to experiencing the truth of things beyond the distortion of conditioning. In his Yoga Sutras, the primary text of Yoga philosophy, Maharishi Patanjali speaks of a level of knowledge called *ritambhara*, or truth-filled perception (I:48). This is a highly refined state of inner perception that enables you to know anything you wish to know, and to experience anything you wish to experience, just as it is, without distortion. Would you like to see the inside of a star, smell a flower never before seen, or know events taking place at a distance? Ritambhara makes this possible.

This pure intuitive knowledge is related to imagination, but acquiring it depends on refining and purifying your body, mind, intellect, and subtle senses through spiritual practices such as meditation. When a high degree of purity in the inner instruments of cognition is gained, and the power of imagination is refined as a result, you may know and experience anything at will within your consciousness. (The next step is the ability to manifest whatever you want.)

This principle has a practical application in meditation. If, for instance, you don't see light at the chakra (or you don't feel the subtle energy-awareness rising up the spine to the chakras as you breathe in), you may gently nudge your experience with your imagination. The keyword here is *gently*. Don't try, don't make an effort — that would be counterproductive because effort keeps your mind at a more superficial level and creates strain, spoiling the meditation. This is a crucial point that can't be emphasized enough: sublime ease is, as ever, the first key to success in meditation. So very gently introduce a faint intention that *easily* engages your imagination. Don't require a clear result. See what comes to you. It is not you who creates the result, but rather the innate creative power of your consciousness that does so, and it may take time for that channel to clear.

When you imagine light at the chakras, at first you may wonder whether you are seeing the light or not; then you may believe you see the light, but wonder whether it is there or you are just imagining it. In time, however, you will see the light spontaneously, at which point it is no longer imagination: through your intention, you have opened to a clearer experience of a subtle level of consciousness.

Another advantage of gently applying your imagination is that this faint intention brings more focus to the chakra. You engage yet more of the brain — not only the areas of the brain related to the sense of sight, but also the areas of the brain related to imagination — which generates a more holistic awareness that is now applied to the chakra. As long as you don't make an effort, this increased focus and holistic awareness will deepen your meditation and accelerate your progress.

But don't make the mistake of thinking meditation is all about imagination. You don't have to *do* meditation by imagining what you want to experience. That's not it at all. Rather, meditation is far more about innocent perception at subtle levels of consciousness; nonetheless, imagination can at times enter into the process to nudge perception. To understand this better, let's try an experiment. (You'll need to read the following through before doing it.)

Close your eyes and very gently think one of the mantras — for instance, Yam (pronounced *Yum*) — at the heart chakra. Think the mantra gently a few times until it begins to fade. You have just experienced the innocent perception of the mantra fading to a more delicate level of consciousness. Now gently imagine Yam at the same faint level. Try going back and forth a few times between imagination and simply thinking the mantra. You may discover that there's not much difference between the two.

Now try this with light in, say, your chest. With eyes closed, first see if you can perceive a faint glow of clear, white light, or perhaps golden light, in the area of your chest. Whether you can or cannot perceive light, now gently imagine light there. One way to do this with ease is to imagine dropping one photon into your chest as a catalyst that effortlessly generates light. Then again see if you innocently perceive the light. Alternate a few times between innocently perceiving light (if it's there for you) and imagining light. Many people find that even if they cannot perceive light at first, after imagining light, the perception of light becomes available.

This exercise raises an interesting question: if your imagination is involved, is what you perceive in meditation real? Well, were the visions of the great mystics real? Certainly imagination played a role in many of their visions. Saint Teresa of Avila experienced ecstatic visions of Christ, and Meerabai (a famous Indian mystic-devotee of the sixteenth century) experienced Krishna; otherwise, in terms of the ecstasy, devotion, and divine union, their experiences were very similar. It may even be said that their imaginations — guided by religious and cultural conditioning — led them to the perception of the Divine. Were their experiences of the Divine real, then? Anyone who has had a clear experience of the Divine, within any tradition, will tell you without a shadow of doubt that what he or she experienced was more real than the world you experience with your senses. The experience of God transcends any possibility of doubt. Certainly also, the mystic's biology is greatly affected by their inner experience: it creates real ecstasy, uplifts emotion, inspires and clears the intellect, and modifies behavior to be, for instance, more compassionate and loving. Can we say this is not real? Imagination is a natural human faculty that can serve human growth every bit as much as intellectual analysis or empathy can.

Most significantly, however, the experience of every mystic, no matter the culture and religion, takes place within awareness. There never has been, nor can there ever be, any conception or experience of the Divine that does not arise within awareness. This points to the truth of the matter: can anything create something greater than itself? Awareness is the source of all conceptions of the Divine, the container of even the most exalted mystical experiences, and yet transcends every experience. It is ever beyond any limitation, ever incomprehensible. Awareness is the Infinite; Godhead is already within you, and that is your own inmost Self.

The point of all this is that awareness is the generator of all mystical experience, and so it is perfectly legitimate to test whether a very gentle nudge from imagination helps you to perceive inner light at each chakra, even if only faintly. If this gentle nudge enhances your experience and you enter deeper into your meditation, great. If it detracts from your experience in any way, this means some effort has crept into the process, and then it's better to ease off and simply enjoy the faint feeling or tone of the mantra at the chakra, or the silence and sense of expansion there, and not worry about experiencing light. The critical point is: don't try. Effort is counterproductive.

I've known many experienced meditators who did not perceive inner light, but who experienced great depth and a vast space of consciousness in their meditations. If that is your experience, embrace it.

STEPS OF THE MEDITATION

1. Sit comfortably and set your intention: "May the merit and benefits of this meditation be multiplied infinitely to bring peace and happiness to all beings." Close your eyes and feel this intention for a few moments. Allow yourself to feel gratitude for the sacred gift of meditation you are about to enjoy.

2. Breathe naturally through the nose. Close your eyes and gently bring your attention to the area of the root chakra, at the perineum. Now, for three or four breaths, practice mulabandha with your breath, firmly contracting the perineum as you inhale and relaxing it as you exhale. With each exhalation, feel a warm expansion at the root chakra, and very gently think "Lam" (pronounced *Lum*, with a short *u*). Feel the mantra in the area of the chakra as a faint idea or feeling, not as a clear mental pronunciation; the fainter the mantra, the better.

3. Cease mulabandha and continue to gently, easily think the mantra Lam a few more times at the root chakra. Let the mantra gradually fade into a faint feeling, steady tone, or silence (any of these is fine). This fading of the mantra will probably happen within a few mental repetitions. If the mantra doesn't fade away on

its own after five or six gentle mental repetitions, just consciously let it go and enjoy the feeling or silence that follows. That feeling or silence will be permeated with the resonance of the mantra created by the repetitions. You may also experience a sense of unboundedness. Just be, savoring the silence or unboundedness at the chakra for ten to fifteen seconds.

4. Gently imagine light at the root chakra. (If you wish, you may imagine dropping one photon into the root chakra as a catalyst that generates light.) However it comes, if it comes, is fine. It may be a faint glow, a clear light, or like the light of a star, the sun, or the moon. That silence or unboundedness and the light are one: the silence, unboundedness, and light of pure being. If light comes, enjoy it for ten to fifteen seconds. If no light comes, this is no cause for concern. If your experience of meditation doesn't involve light, then simply savor the silence at the chakra. If you feel a spacelike unboundedness there, you may let your awareness merge into that unboundedness at the chakra.

5. Again for three or four breaths, perform mulabandha as you inhale, and draw your awareness into the base of the spine at your tailbone (the site of your sacral chakra). As you exhale, feel a sense of warm expansion at your tailbone and very gently think "Vam" (pronounced *Vum*). Feel the mantra in the sacral chakra.

6. Cease mulabandha and continue to gently, easily think the mantra Vam a few more times at the sacral chakra. Let the mantra dissolve into a faint feeling or tone

and then into silence. Just be. Enjoy this silence in the sacral chakra for ten to fifteen seconds.

7. Gently imagine light at the sacral chakra. Simply be, enjoying the light (or, if no light comes, the silence) for ten to fifteen seconds. If you feel silent, spacelike unboundedness at the chakra, enjoy that.

8. Now repeat this for each chakra in turn. At the navel chakra, use the mantra Ram (pronounced *Rum*), letting it dissolve into silence-light-unboundedness. In time, at each chakra, you may experience the silence, light, and unboundedness simultaneously, rather than as separate steps. This is entirely appropriate; what you are experiencing is the silence, light, and unboundedness of pure being, the Self. If they come together, just enjoy the experience for ten to twenty seconds and continue to the next chakra.

9. At the heart chakra, use Yam (pronounced *Yum*). Then silence-light-unboundedness.

10. At the throat chakra, use Ham (pronounced *Hum*). Then silence-light-unboundedness.

11. At the third-eye chakra, use Om (pronounced *Om*). Then silence-light-unboundedness.

12. At the crown center, just allow your awareness to be at first absorbed in transcendent silence at the crown of the head, and then feel there an orb of clear light, like the sun or a transcendent full moon. Let your awareness be absorbed in that light. Sit in that absorbed state for a minute or more. If you don't experience any light, allow your awareness to be absorbed in whatever inner silence and unboundedness you feel at your

crown. Then very gently be aware of and feel the subtle light and blissful energy that are now permeating your body.

13. If you have time and you wish to continue meditating, you can bring your attention back to the root chakra at the perineum and go through the chakras again. If you do so, you may wish to omit mulabandha this time. Feel free to improvise. For instance, you might now briefly go through the chakras again and enjoy the faint vibration of the mantras at each chakra. Then you could go through the chakras again and enjoy light at each chakra. Follow your bliss; play with it. Whatever deepens your experience is good, and you'll gradually become adept at moving your attention at those fine, powerful levels of consciousness.

14. End the meditation by lying down in the corpse pose for no less than five minutes to come out slowly.

15. Finally, before you get up, close your meditation with an expression of gratitude and set an intention for the day to be an instrument in the hands of the Divine: "Thank you for this life, my wife [or husband], my family, this beautiful earth, my job [and so on — name whatever you feel grateful for]. May I be an instrument of healing and peace in your hands."

As your practice of chakra meditation continues, you will find that by this meditation, you enter into a state of expansive, deep, and silent pure awareness. This is the experience of your innermost essence, your higher, blissful Self. Though it is often described in exalted terms by the mystics of the world's great spiritual traditions, you will find it takes place in an entirely natural and easy way. You may enjoy that state of absorption for as long as it is compelling. It will have a profoundly opening, energizing, and healing effect on the mind, heart, and body. And as you purify your inner faculties of perception through regular meditation, you will begin to appreciate the exquisite bliss that is your innermost nature.

Congratulations. You have completed the final stage of chakra meditation. This meditation will powerfully awaken the spiritual energies in your body and direct those energies upward, clearing the nadis, opening the chakras, and balancing the elements in your body. As a result, you are likely to notice increased alertness, energy, and vitality; improved health; and greater creativity, inner strength, joy, and love. Gradually, the light of your higher Self will shine brighter to support all aspects of your life.

CHAPTER 6

CENTERED
IN THE HEART

Now that you have begun to awaken the subtle energies and open and clear your chakras, you are ready to learn the next phase of Effortless Mind meditation: meditation in the heart center. The chakra meditation you have already learned clears the path for the experience of abiding in the Self, in pure awareness, and in the process brings great energy, vitality, clarity, and focus. Mantra meditation in the heart center gives you a slightly different angle: it allows you to more gradually traverse the full range of the mind, from the conscious thinking level, through all the subtler layers of the mind, to pure awareness, where you rest in the inner abode that is the Self of joy, peace, and love.

The benefits of mantra meditation in the heart center are many. First, daily traversing all the layers of the mind will enlarge your capacity to use more of your mind outside of meditation. This makes for a qualitative difference in your thinking: The deeper layers of thought are more abstract, not so rigidly bound, so thought at deeper levels is more expansive and all-encompassing. You will begin to see more vividly that all is interconnected; black-and-white thinking becomes a thing of the past.

Those quieter layers of thought are also brimming with creative energy. Many great scientists and artists have noted that their greatest discoveries came not while they struggled to solve a problem but while they were relaxed and quiet — taking a shower, for instance, or walking on the beach, or sipping a cup of tea. In that relaxed state, they found that suddenly and unexpectedly the answer came in a flash. Why is this such a frequently related experience? Because focused effort to solve a problem engages the subconscious mind, which can then yield great insight when you are in a settled, receptive state. Meditation will give you systematic access to those more expansive, creative levels of the mind. Not only will you find aha moments occurring more frequently in your life, but gradually you will also begin to use those deeper levels of your mind consciously, resulting in greater creativity and an expanded, more holistic perspective.

This meditation is also very relaxing, and so it is an excellent remedy for stress and all the effects of stress, such as insomnia, anxiety, depression, and stress-related illness. And, as you might expect, mantra meditation in the heart center will also open your heart, opening you to greater empathy and love.

OPENING THE HEART

What does it mean to open your heart, and how does this meditation accomplish it? First, as you transcend and experience subtler states of the mantra through meditation, all your faculties — your hearing, sight, taste, touch, and smell — are refined, as are your heart and intellect. This develops your capacity to appreciate the world and people around you (and as we shall see, appreciation is intimately linked to love). When you emerge from meditation, colors may look brighter, the air may seem crystalline, smells are more fragrant, tastes are more delicious, your mind is sharpened and clear, and your heart is opened to more delicate feelings. It's not uncommon following a deep meditation to spontaneously feel love for not only those close to you but also for everyone and everything. This is a function of refined perception and refined feeling, allowing you to appreciate everything at a deeper level, which spontaneously opens your heart.

Consider young lovers: to the extent that they abound in appreciation for each other, they feel that wonderful fresh bloom of romantic love. Someone looking on from the outside may not see what they see in each other; the couple's appreciation is a subtle perception and feeling. It is not obvious to everyone. This experience is not limited to young love. Even in mature relationships, the deepest feelings of love come when you are quiet, looking into each other's eyes, seeing beyond the obvious into the very soul of your partner. Seeing the depths of your partner is a subtle perception that spontaneously opens your heart. By refining all your faculties and unfolding your innocence, meditation will gradually develop your appreciation and love for everything and everyone. You will naturally begin to feel unconditional, universal love, usually considered the hallmark of spiritual development.

This is one reason meditation in some form or another lies at the heart of nearly every great spiritual tradition of the world. The spiritual truth of life is subtle. It is not seen on the obvious, gross level of life. To live a deep and vital spirituality, we must make our minds and hearts extremely subtle, open to the most delicate feelings and perceptions. As Christ put it: "You will listen and listen again, but not understand, see and see again, but not perceive. For the heart of this nation has grown coarse, their ears are dull of hearing, and they have shut their eyes, for fear they should see with their eyes, hear with their ears, understand with their heart."

By making your mind and all your faculties more subtle, this meditation will allow you to see truly, hear truly, understand truly, with the innocence of a child. That is the key to opening the heart and to developing spiritual experience.

Secondly, this meditation is focused on the area of the center of the chest, the heart center. Bringing your awareness to rest here while transcending to deeper, more powerful levels will also open your heart. This unfolds a world of delicate and sublime feeling — supreme compassion, devotion, and divine love — as well as indescribable states of ecstasy.

DEVI PRANAVA

Having learned chakra meditation, you're already familiar with mantras and how to use them. Still, as a refresher, you may wish to reread the beginning of chapter 4, where I discuss what mantras are. Thoroughly understanding the proper use of mantras will help ensure your success in the heart-centered mantra meditation.

The mantra you will use in this meditation is an especially powerful one for positive life-affirming transformation. It is the mantra Hrim (pronounced *Hreem*). In some of India's spiritual texts, this mantra is called Devi Pranava. *Devi* refers to the feminine Divine, the Goddess. *Pranava* is a term denoting Om (or AUM), the primordial vibration from which all other vibrations emerge. So the Devi Pranava is extolled as the equivalent of Om, which is declared in the Upanishads to be the supreme mantra. But whereas Om represents the silent, unmanifest principle, Devi Pranava represents the principle of creative, nurturing, loving energy.

Now you may wonder: if Om is such a great mantra, why not just use it for meditating? The answer to this question is very interesting and illustrates the vibratory effects of mantras.

As the primordial vibration, Om is the vibration preceding the first expression of creation. It is as close as a vibration can come to the unmanifest state of pure being. Were you to continually meditate on Om, continually resonate in that vibration of the unmanifest, your life would begin to reflect the character of the unmanifest. You would find yourself drawn strongly inward, away from active engagement in the world. You would also find that possessions and relations would tend to drop away from you; your vibration would neither attract nor sustain worldly objects and interests. This is an example of the transformative power of pure vibration.

Om is, in fact, a perfect mantra for those who want little or nothing to do with the world, who wish to withdraw from the world and renounce distractions from their spiritual path, such as home, intimate relationships, family, and career. That is, it's the perfect mantra for monks and nuns in contemplative traditions, which is why Om is a prevalent mantra in traditions of India that have come to favor renunciation of "worldly life" as an ideal.

Devi Pranava is said to equate to Om in excellence, but the term *Devi* indicates that its vibration *embraces* creation, as a mother her child, with love and nurturing. This mantra vibrates with the Infinite but also nurtures you in the highest values of creation: love, joy, creativity, dynamism, prosperity, and so on. As a loving mother wants to see her child fulfilled in every way, so Devi Pranava supports both spiritual development and prosperity and success in the world. Its goal is both spiritual *and* material abundance. Devi Pranava is an ideal mantra for those who not only want to realize the Infinite Self but also wish to express their creative potential through active life.

These two mantras, then, are for two entirely different paths: Om is for the path of renunciation (*samnyasa* yoga), and Devi Pranava (and other *devi* mantras; there are many) is for the path of active engagement in the world (karma yoga). Both paths are valid. Both paths ultimately lead to the same inner goal — union with the Divine — though the two lifestyles differ dramatically. Obviously, for the vast majority of humanity, the path of active engagement in the world is more appropriate. Because Devi Pranava also supports the ideal of divine love, it is the ideal mantra for meditation on the heart center. I should add that the minute or two a day one spends meditating on Om at the ajna chakra during the chakra meditation will certainly not have a deleterious effect on those on the path of action. It will strengthen discernment and refine perception, which are also needed, even on the path of the heart.

Pranava also means "that by which the pranas are quieted to merge into the Self." Yogis identify ten distinct pranas that serve different functions in the body. Were the ten pranas to leave your body, you would die. During meditation on Pranava (Om) or Devi Pranava (or on any mantra conducive to transcendence), the pranas do not leave your body — they are simply calmed and settled into their source, your own innermost Self, pure consciousness, from which all activity arises.

Previously we discussed transcending in mental terms, as a process of coming to quieter or subtler states of thought. The process of quieting the pranas is another perspective on transcending. Recall from chapter 2 the close interrelationship between the physical body, the energetic or pranic body, and the mind. When the pranas are active, bodily processes are also active, and the mind operates on the superficial conscious level. As the pranas settle to rest in their source, the Self, they become far less active. The mantra, which is the vehicle for transcendence, settles the pranas into their source. As a result, the functions of the body are minimized, and the mind correspondingly settles into its essential nature, pure awareness.

Now let's directly experience settling the pranas by meditating on the heart center using Devi Pranava.

STEPS OF THE MEDITATION

Read the following steps through before actually meditating. In fact, you may want to read the steps through several times so you are thoroughly familiar with them before closing your eyes to meditate.

1. Sit comfortably and set your intention: "May the merit and benefits of this meditation be multiplied infinitely to bring peace and happiness to all beings." Close your eyes and feel this intention for a few moments. Allow yourself to feel gratitude for the sacred gift of meditation you are about to enjoy.

2. Do your chakra meditation. This will set the stage for you to have a deeper, clearer experience of meditating on your heart center.

3. Once you've finished your chakra meditation, allow your awareness to effortlessly rest in the center of your chest — let it be a very light, easy, abstract awareness. You need not visualize anything or feel any distinct sensation, just a gentle, faint awareness resting in the heart center.

4. Begin to easily think the Devi Pranava mantra, which is Hrim (pronounced *Hreem*), without expectation or effort. Remember, even at the conscious level, thought is not a clear pronunciation, and meditation will take the mantra to deeper, more abstract levels, so don't try to think the mantra clearly and don't worry about pronunciation. That would only interfere with the process. Allow the mantra to dissolve as you mentally repeat it very easily. Allow it to become just a faint feeling, or perhaps you will feel it as a faint, steady tone. Simply enjoy this.

5. You will have thoughts; they are a part of the process. Let them go as they come without minding them. Just return to the mantra at a fine level, with your awareness still resting in the area of the heart center. Think

"Hrim" gently and allow it to dissolve to a faint feeling or tone.

6. If at any time your awareness strays from the general area of the heart center, gently bring it back. Resting in the heart center is a faint, effortless awareness. If it's not effortless to allow your awareness to rest at the heart center, just enjoy the mantra wherever it is, or enjoy it even if it seems to have no relationship with your body. This will still be an effective meditation. It won't be long before you find it easy to rest in the heart center, but in the meantime, just enjoy whatever comes easily.

7. Continue to meditate in this way for three to eight minutes, depending on how much time you want to allot to meditation. Don't bother timing the meditation, and don't worry about going a little longer if it happens. Finish when you feel like you want to.

8. End the meditation by lying down in the corpse pose for five minutes to come out slowly.

9. Finally, before you get up, close your meditation with an expression of gratitude and set an intention for the day to be an instrument in the hands of the Divine: "Thank you for this life, my wife [or husband], my family, this beautiful earth, my job [and so on — name whatever you feel grateful for]. May I be an instrument of healing and peace in your hands."

Congratulations. You have just had your first experience of heart-centered mantra meditation. Make a mental note of your experience. Was it peaceful? Did it seem to go on almost by itself, without effort? Did you have lots of thoughts? If you did, that is entirely fine. (We'll talk more about thoughts in meditation in chapter 9.) What else did you notice? Did your breathing become fainter? Did you feel any sensations in your chest? How about deep stillness or silence, moments of sweetness or love, expansion of awareness? Any one of these is an indication of successful meditation. You may wish to keep a journal of your experiences in meditation. This can help deepen your meditation and support your regular practice.

WHAT WAS THAT?

By now you may have had one experience that I haven't yet described. Many people experience this during either the chakra meditation or the heart-centered mantra meditation. I'm speaking of the experience of, well, no experience. That is, a point where you realize that you were neither thinking thoughts nor practicing the meditation, and you're pretty sure you weren't asleep. Have you had such an experience, even if only momentarily?

This happens when you transcend the subtlest state of thought. You are still aware, but there is no object of awareness. You are simply abiding in awareness itself. The reason it seems to be an absence of experience is that it is just that; there is no object of experience. However, as you gain more clarity at subtle levels of awareness over time, you'll begin to appreciate this state of simply abiding in your innermost Self, the state of pure awareness. Simply practice with patience, without expectation, and gradually you will find that it is a state of indescribably blissful unboundedness, wholeness, clear light, and pure intelligence.

CHAPTER 7

HEALTH AND
LONG LIFE

You may have heard legends of yogis high in the pristine snows of the Himalayas who have, over many decades of long meditation, extended their life spans to an unbelievable extent. These yogis are supposed to have refined the very cells of their bodies into the light of consciousness, or so lore has it, and I have spoken to native people of the Himalayas who swear they have seen these yogis with bodies made of light.

Such claims may seem difficult to swallow. Nonetheless, if you practice the meditations in this book, you will directly experience the principles on which such legends are based. Meditate daily, and you will feel your body filled with and held by powerful yet soothing light and energy (prana), and your cells invigorated, enlivened, and protected by that light and energy. What's more, meditate daily and you may not only live longer, but perhaps more importantly, you may enjoy a better quality of life in your old age.

Even the Western scientific research on meditation suggests this possibility: stress is a recognized factor in many illnesses, including potentially deadly ones like cancer and cardiovascular disease, and meditation is widely accepted as an effective stress-management tool. For that reason alone, chances are that your health will fare better if you are a meditator. Also, those who meditate may live longer on average. In fact, in one recent study, meditation was found to significantly increase telomerase activity (a predictor of long-term cellular viability), suggesting enhanced immune cell longevity. Further, research has shown that certain aspects of aging, such as cognitive decline and impaired cardiovascular functions, are mitigated by meditation. This may hardly be a promise of immortality, but at least such benefits should help you feel younger and healthier as you do age — and you'll probably live longer as well.

Though Western science has yet to prove that meditation lengthens a person's life span, yogic science has long held out this potential. It's worth taking a few minutes to understand this possibility from the traditional yogic perspective.

TRANSFORMING THE LAYERS OF YOUR BEING

According to the science of Yoga, there are five layers to your being. These are called the five sheaths, or *pancha koshas* (*pancha* means "five," and *kosha* means "sheath"), that cover your innermost Self. The five sheaths are as follows:

- THE SHEATH OF FOOD (*annamaya kosha*). This refers to the physical body.

- THE SHEATH OF PRANA (*pranamaya kosha*). Prana is life force, or subtle energy: the pranic body, or energetic body, includes the entire system of prana and seventy-two thousand subtle channels (nadis) through which prana flows in the body.

- THE SHEATH OF MIND (*manomaya kosha*). This refers to the thinking mind, which includes not only thoughts but also emotions, desires, and motivations, both conscious and subconscious.

- THE SHEATH OF INTELLECT OR WISDOM (*vijnanamaya kosha*). This refers to the refined intellect that apprehends abstract principles and higher knowledge and truths.

- THE SHEATH OF BLISS (*anandamaya kosha*). This is a delicate level of your being, the nature of which is intense bliss. It is the blissful layer of a person (invisible to most because it is so fine) that veils the pure, transcendent Self.

Beyond these five sheaths, the core of your being shines — unbounded, infinite, immortal pure awareness. The science of Yoga holds that through spiritual practices, particularly meditation, all these layers of your being are purified. As they are purified, more of the nature of your innermost Self shines through, enlivening divine ecstasy in the sheath of bliss; illuminating your intellect with profound truth; healing, soothing, and calming your mind while restoring the innocence of your opened heart; optimizing and balancing the flow of subtle energies; and healing and normalizing the functioning of your physical body. This is the yogic view of the benefits of meditation on the five layers (sheaths) of your being.

These benefits are ordinarily thought to culminate with enlightenment. What is enlightenment? I discuss this further in chapter 10, but essentially it amounts to gaining such clarity through the purification of the sheaths (particularly the intellect-wisdom sheath) that a recognition dawns: "I am not my body; I am not my mind or my intellect; I am That, the Infinite." And this recognition may further extend to recognizing: "I am the Self of all." For the innermost essence of you is the innermost essence of me and of all things. We are all part of a great, divine unity. So teaches the Vedantic system of Indian philosophy.

This description only scratches the surface of enlightenment, but the point here is this: What if, through intensive practice, the process of purification of the sheaths could continue, allowing more and more of the value of infinite pure awareness to illuminate all of the sheaths? Pure awareness, being entirely abstract and nonmaterial, is pure Spirit. It is boundless, infinite, blissful, and immortal. If every layer and even every cell of your being could be suffused by your highest Self, could your physical body perhaps take on the character of infinity, of immortality?

Such a transmutation of the physical body is perceived as a real possibility in the yogic traditions of both India and Tibet. In Tibet, they call this attainment the "Body of Glory" or the "Rainbow Body" (*jai-lus*) — a transmuted body consisting of spiritual light in which one also attains such abilities as becoming invisible at will. Even the Judeo-Christian tradition suggests such a possibility: not only did Christ, postresurrection, have a body of light, but purportedly so did the Old Testament prophet Elijah.

Whether you believe in this possibility or not, the essential principle of transformation through meditation is important to understand: it occurs where spiritual consciousness intersects with the relative layers of your being (the koshas). Consciousness, your inmost Self, is already unbounded and free. No transformation at the level of consciousness is needed, and none can take place there. Consciousness in itself is already pure. However, to realize that fact, to enjoy and live it, you must purify and illuminate the koshas; this is the key to personal growth. All growth, any transformation of any kind, takes place on the level of the koshas only, not on the level of the Self.

This is why all the meditations I teach connect consciousness with the koshas. So far, the meditations you've learned have connected consciousness primarily with the energetic, mental, intellectual, and bliss koshas. The relaxing and purifying effects on the physical body have been significant but incidental. Now we are going to specifically direct consciousness to the level of the physical body, to the annamaya kosha. You'll appreciate the difference once you actually do the meditation.

Transforming the physical body so that it might last hundreds of years may be a far-fetched goal, but you can still apply this principle to profound effect. The more your koshas imbibe prana and the bliss of the Self, the clearer, lighter, happier, healthier, and more energized and peaceful your mind and body will be. That's a worthwhile goal in any case; if your body stays vital longer, so much the better. The meditation you will learn in this chapter is designed to infuse your body with the influence of immortality, of your Self.

I should note first that really you are not the body or mind or any of the sheaths that we all identify with. You are the Self, infinite, ever free. You, the essence of you, are already immortal. Realize this, and live that eternal freedom. That, ultimately, is the goal of meditation.

STEPS OF THE MEDITATION

Please read the following steps before actually meditating. When you feel you understand the flow of the steps, you are ready to start.

1. Sit comfortably, close your eyes, and set your intention: "May the merit and benefits of this meditation be multiplied infinitely to bring peace and happiness to all beings." Close your eyes and feel this intention for a few moments. Allow yourself to feel gratitude for the sacred gift of meditation you are about to enjoy.

2. Do your chakra meditation and then your heart-centered mantra meditation. These meditations bring your attention to a subtle and powerful level so that the meditation for health and longevity will be more profound. Without these, it will not be nearly so effective. This is an important factor that differentiates this meditation from similar body-scan techniques.

3. Once you've finished the chakra and heart meditations, allow your awareness to effortlessly rest on your feet — let it be a very light, easy, abstract awareness. You don't need to visualize your feet or feel any distinct sensation there; rather, just delicately bathe your feet in the same subtle awareness you experienced during your heart-centered mantra meditation. Don't anticipate any particular experience. Simply caress your feet gently with your awareness. While doing this, faintly think (this can be just a faint feeling) the mantra Hrim (pronounced *Hreem*) once, bathing your feet in the pure vibration of that mantra. The vibration of the mantra from your heart meditation already saturates your awareness, so all that's needed is just the slightest impulse to enliven it — the fainter, the better.

4. After five to ten seconds, gently move your awareness to your ankles and calves. Again, feel the mantra Hrim as a faint background tone, effortlessly bathing your ankles and calves in that pure vibration.

5. Continue like this, spending five to ten seconds caressing each area of your body with delicate, blissful awareness and the faint background feeling of the mantra: your knees, your thighs, your hips, seat, and pelvic area (as one or separately; your choice), your lower torso (stomach and lower back), your middle torso, your upper torso (chest and upper back), your hands, your wrists and forearms, your upper arms, your shoulders, your neck and throat, and your head.

Enjoy the awareness of each part of the body. Be aware that you are healing those areas with the soothing vibration of the mantra while suffusing them with powerful, blissful, pure awareness.

6. Now gently be aware of your whole body. Feel the subtle light and blissful energy that permeate your body. You don't have to imagine or visualize anything; just feel the light and energy that are already there. Enjoy this for as long as you like, up to about a minute.

7. End the meditation by lying in the corpse pose for no less than five minutes to come out slowly.

8. Finally, before you get up, close your meditation with an expression of gratitude and set an intention for the day to be an instrument in the hands of the Divine.

Congratulations. You have just completed the meditation for health and longevity. The secret to success in this meditation is an easy, light, faint awareness and receptivity. That is, don't try for a particular experience as you go through the parts of your body — don't try to visualize or push for a vivid experience of your body. Just be very easy with it. Also, don't go passively from one body part to another with a ho-hum attitude. Quietly relish the feeling of your awareness and the subtle background feeling of the mantra bathing or caressing each area of the body. You may also find that you spontaneously feel subtle light bathing each area of the body.

Once you become comfortable with this meditation and it feels entirely easy and enjoyable to you, you can vary it. When doing your torso, for instance, you can also choose to be aware of your internal organs: your intestines, stomach, liver, spleen, kidneys, and heart. You can also try starting at the crown of your head and moving down the body instead of up from the feet. Whichever way works best for you is perfect.

AMRIT: THE NECTAR OF IMMORTALITY

One final practice will complete your meditation for health and longevity. This is an exquisite technique designed to help develop the "biochemistry of enlightenment." It directs consciousness to the bliss sheath (the subtlest sheath) primarily, but its effects cascade to purify all layers of your being.

According to the Tantric texts of India, when, during meditation, the spiritual energy (Kundalini Shakti) rises up the primary nadi in the center of the spine (*shushumna*) to the crown of the head, the meditator experiences indescribable bliss and divine union. This is represented symbolically as the union of Shiva and Shakti. (Shiva is universal pure awareness, the Absolute, conceived of as the divine masculine; Shiva is also the destroyer, which allows something new to arise. Shakti is the active, creative power of the Absolute, which is conceived of as the divine feminine.) From their union at the crown of the head flows the "nectar of immortality," or Amrit, showering down and imbuing the meditator with strength, vigor, and intelligence.

This is typically understood to represent the moment of enlightenment: the immense spiritual power that lies latent within you rises up the shushumna to merge at the crown with Shiva (your Self, pure consciousness). When that happens, your ego-mind dissolves into the blissful fullness of divine universal consciousness, and voilà! Enlightenment! However, this symbolic representation also applies each and every time you transcend into pure awareness, even right now, as a new meditator. In fact, it offers deep insight into what is happening in the subtler layers of your being, whether you are momentarily transcending or gaining enlightenment.

Whenever you experience what you might consider a really "deep" meditation, it is because spiritual energy, prana (referred to here as Shakti), awakens through your meditation and spontaneously moves up the shushumna nadi in your spine. (You need not be focused on this energy for it to awaken and rise; this can, for instance, take place during the heart-centered mantra meditation as well as during the chakra meditation.) If that spiritual energy rises all the way to the crown of your head, you will spontaneously abide in pure awareness, even if just for a few moments.

Now, as a beginning meditator, all the spiritual power has not yet awakened within you, so only a trickle of Shakti reaches your crown. Consequently, your experience of that union, pure awareness, while pleasant and deeply restful, is a shadow of the full experience of ecstatic union in the Divine. Nonetheless, even that shadow confers great benefit.

So where does Amrit come into this? Amrit is the finest aspect of the "biochemistry" of pure awareness. Consider this: every significant change in our consciousness is accompanied by biochemical changes in the body. When you are angry, for instance, biochemical changes take place in your body. You can feel the effects of some of these: your face flushes, your muscles tense, and so on. Likewise, when you are anxious or fearful, you feel the effects of the accompanying biochemical changes: your palms moisten, your mouth becomes dry, and your stomach may be queasy. Biochemical changes also take place when you transcend into pure awareness. The effects you feel depend on the degree of clarity of your inner perception and may range from deep relaxation, inner stillness, and a sense of well-being to ecstatic bliss. Amrit is the underlying "biochemistry" of these experiences.

The reason I put *biochemistry* in quotes when referring to Amrit is because, though biochemical changes definitely take place in the body during meditation, and though these changes are related to the flow of Amrit, no biochemist will ever find this nectar of immortality in the physical body. Rather, Amrit is a synergistic phenomenon experienced at the level of the bliss sheath (anandamaya kosha). Nonetheless, as your subtle perception becomes clear, you will vividly experience the flow of Amrit, and the effects of Amrit flowing in your sheath of bliss will profoundly affect every level of your being.

In order to give you a better picture of the benefits, here is a description of the range of what happens to the koshas through the "union of Shiva and Shakti" — that is, through transcendence into pure awareness, even if only momentarily, and the resulting flow of Amrit. First I'll describe the full effect on a given kosha, or layer of your being, which you might feel after some years of regularly practicing meditation, and following that I'll describe the effect you will likely notice when first beginning to meditate.

- In your *sheath of bliss* you delight in the flow of Amrit, the blissful nectar of immortality, which falls in a pure stream from the crown of your head, imbuing you with divine ecstasy.

In someone new to meditation, this will likely not be felt clearly, but the flow of Amrit is taking place nonetheless and will result in pleasant feelings in the mind and body.

- The *sheath of intellect/wisdom* is illuminated by universal, divine intelligence. The meditator may be fulfilled in a state of all-knowingness.

In the beginning, insights and revelations are common.

- The *sheath of mind* is exalted to a state of superconsciousness, utter fulfillment, peace, and divine love. The heart opens to delicate, sublime levels of feeling and universal love.

In the beginning, you will feel increased alertness and a sense of relaxation, ease, and well-being. You may also experience more — for instance, many of my students, even those new to meditation, have described feelings of universal love following a deep meditation.

- The *sheath of prana* is vitalized and opened. All the pranas are awakened to flow in balance, resulting in lightness of body, optimal health, physical bliss, and vitality. The meditator's countenance shines with an inner radiance.

In the beginning, you will experience increased energy, clarity, and a sense of balance and health in the body, mind, and emotions.

- The biochemistry of the *sheath of the physical body* is

profoundly purified, every cell enlivened and awakened, and one may taste a sweetness that is the sign of Amrit flowing, as well as exude a sublime fragrance that others may notice. The "biochemistry of enlightenment" is developing.

In the beginning, you will gain greater energy, clarity, and improved health. Your senses will be strengthened, and you may notice that after a deep meditation, colors seem brighter and the air crystalline, food tastes better, and music and the sounds of nature seem more beautiful.

So, as you meditate, you are already ripening — gradually awakening subtle energies, opening the nadis, purifying and healing the koshas, gaining more and more inner clarity, and enjoying greater inner peace, joy, and all the other benefits of meditation. Every time you transcend into pure awareness, you stimulate the flow of Amrit — whether you perceive it or not — cascading within the sheath of bliss. Its effects are felt by all the sheaths as it enlivens and reinforces the innate intelligence governing the functioning of all the layers of your being and of all your faculties. As you continue to meditate and purify the subtle layers of your own consciousness, the process of transcending becomes clearer, and the quality of Amrit increases. Eventually, the faculties become so refined and sharp that one perceives the Divine within everything, through one's senses, heart, and intellect. Enlightenment comes all at once, but the ripeness for God-realization develops over many years of practice and integration.

The ripening I've described is the natural path of spiritual evolution — gradual, safe, and comfortable. It bears mentioning that personal growth through spiritual practices is not always so smooth. Perhaps you have heard the term *kundalini crisis*. This occurs when a burst of spiritual power (Shakti) is stimulated prematurely, usually through forceful means such as intensive breathing exercises or other intense yogic practices. If the sheaths have not been adequately purified by years of regular spiritual practice, attempting a shortcut to enlightenment can cause rapid purification that is uncomfortable and may unbalance the body, mind, and emotions. This is another reason I teach effortless, gentle practice. Not only is it generally far more effective, but also you will stimulate only what your sheaths are ready for, gradually purifying and preparing all layers of your being for the influx of the Divine.

MANIFESTING AMRIT

Though some Amrit is produced naturally every time you transcend into pure awareness, you may gently increase the flow of Amrit and so begin to enjoy its blissful benefits to a greater degree. This is a wonderful blessing that accelerates all the benefits of meditation.

The technique of increasing the flow of Amrit could not be simpler. You simply think the word *Amrit* for about twenty seconds, allowing it to gradually dissolve into inner silence. When it has dissolved, let the repetition of it go completely and simply *be*, effortlessly aware of your whole body. In effect, you are delicately stirring your own higher Self to manifest the nectar of immortality. Your individual ego-mind does not have the power to manifest Amrit. So you must leave it to your higher Self, which is one with Cosmic Intelligence. Your thought of Amrit, dissolving into the Self, stirs that Cosmic Intelligence to respond by producing the experience of Amrit.

In chapter 5, I briefly mentioned ritambhara, or truth-filled perception, which is discussed in the Yoga Sutras (I:48). Invoking Amrit is another application of ritambhara. Through this technique, you learn to manifest from the source of creation, the deepest level of your own silent consciousness.

STEPS OF THE MEDITATION

Manifesting Amrit takes only a few moments, and the technique for doing so is integrated into the meditations you've already learned. Note that it is not to be used as a mantra for any length of time; just a taste of the celestial nectar of Amrit is sufficient.

The first place in your routine where you may manifest Amrit is after you've enjoyed the light or the space of consciousness at the sahasrara (crown center) at the end of the chakra meditation. You have guided the spiritual energy up the shushumna to the crown of the head — where Shakti unites with Shiva, resulting in the flow of Amrit. Now gently assist this process by manifesting Amrit. Just think "Amrit," as if it were a mantra, for twenty seconds or so, allowing it to gradually dissolve. When it has dissolved, let it go completely; don't continue thinking it. Rather, just *be*, effortlessly and gently aware of your whole body for another twenty to thirty seconds or so. Be open and receptive to what's happening in your body, especially between the head and the heart.

Don't anticipate or push for any particular experience. Just be creatively receptive with childlike innocence.

The second place to manifest Amrit is at the very end of the meditation for health and longevity, after you've felt the light and blissful energy permeating your body. After manifesting Amrit at this point, you can enjoy the blissful feelings in your body for twenty to sixty seconds before lying down to come out of meditation. This technique, in combination with the body-scan meditation for health and longevity, will help to keep you vital, balanced, healthy, and growing in the experience of immortal bliss.

CHAPTER 8

MAKING THE MOST OF YOUR MEDITATION

You have now learned all aspects of Effortless Mind meditation. By this point you very likely have already experienced some of the benefits of meditation — greater relaxation, clarity of mind, and a growing sense of inner peace and well-being, to name just a few. Hopefully, you are ready to establish a daily practice. Before you set out on your own across the vast, uncharted regions of inner space, however, let's go over a number of practical points you may be wondering about: how long to meditate, when to meditate, where to meditate, how to get the most from your meditation, and other frequently asked questions.

HOW LONG SHOULD YOU MEDITATE?

Now that you've learned the chakra meditation with mantra and light, mantra meditation in the heart center, the meditation for health and longevity, and manifesting Amrit, you may feel like this is a lot to do. But keep in mind that you are just learning. You will quickly become more comfortable with the techniques, and as you do you'll gain more fluidity. Your attention will flow from one step of the practice to the next automatically, in considerably less time than it probably takes you now. For instance, in the chakra meditation, you may find that the mantra will fade into silence in a few repetitions, and the silence and light may be simultaneous. In that case, one minute on each chakra is plenty. As you become more proficient, you'll simply go through the steps and, ideally, you'll probably find your entire meditation lasts about twenty to twenty-five minutes, including three to five minutes or so to come out of meditation slowly. That's an optimal length of time for most people. However, if your schedule simply doesn't allow you to take that much time, you can spend a little less time on each portion of the meditation and complete your meditation in as little as fifteen minutes. If you don't have even that much time, you can skip some portion of the meditation and focus on just your favorite, in which case you may need only ten minutes to meditate. Even meditating five minutes is better than no meditation at all. In other words, decide up front how much time you can give yourself to meditate. If you have to shorten or even cut out some portion of the meditation, do so, and then lavishly enjoy your meditation for the allotted time. Don't worry about getting everything in.

Even if you have plenty of time, I wouldn't recommend meditating longer than thirty minutes to begin with. This meditation is highly effective, and too much of a good thing, even meditation, can be unbalancing. We'll talk more about that in the next chapter, on purification.

Just to give you a very rough idea, here are approximate amounts of time you might spend on each step of meditation — though please don't take these too literally. I wouldn't want you to feel bound to a tight schedule in your meditation; rather, relax your sense of time and let your own inner experience determine the amount of time you spend on each part.

- Opening intention for the peace and happiness of all beings: fifteen to thirty seconds
- Chakra meditation with mantra and light: about one minute for each chakra, so about seven minutes
- Manifesting Amrit: one minute or so
- Mantra meditation in the heart center: three to eight minutes
- Body scan, including feeling the light throughout the body: one and a half to three minutes
- Manifesting Amrit: one minute or so
- Lying in the corpse pose to come out of meditation slowly: three to five minutes

If you add these times up, they amount to about seventeen to twenty-five minutes, including the time spent on coming out of meditation.

PRACTICE WITH PATIENCE

While we're on the topic of how long to meditate, a word on patience. If you're as busy as most people I know, the temptation may easily arise in meditation to do what you do in the rest of your day: act efficiently and hurry to get it done so you can move on to the next thing. I fully appreciate the desire to be efficient, but when it comes to meditation, efficiency depends largely on patience. That is, in order to get the most out of your time spent sitting, approach meditation with relaxed, patient mindfulness. This means resisting the temptation to hurry through the steps of meditation.

Meditation is a rare chance to step out of the hustle and bustle of your daily life. It is a chance to be in the moment and relish every nuance of inner experience. So enjoy this opportunity; take your time. (It is *your* time.) In the chakra meditation, for instance, give each chakra its full due, as if it's the only thing in the world for you to be doing. There is nothing else in this moment. Savor the experience. In this way you will go much deeper. Your experience will be richer and juicier. If you find yourself hurrying, simply slow down and focus on enjoying each moment of your meditation without expectation or anticipation. If you need to come out of meditation before finishing all the steps, that's okay. At least you've made the most of the time you did spend meditating.

WHEN SHOULD YOU MEDITATE?

There are just a few basic principles to consider when deciding when to meditate. After that, do what best fits into your daily routine. Here are some things to keep in mind.

Start Your Day with Meditation

Meditation helps you to connect with your higher Self and with deeper, more creative levels of consciousness. It calms you and sets you up to be more creative, more efficient, and better attuned with your higher Self in your activities, so that your actions bring the greatest benefit to yourself and others. For these reasons, it's a good idea to meditate right at the start of your day, so that everything you do afterwards benefits from your meditation. Try not to wait until you're well into your day to meditate. It will be harder to interrupt whatever you're doing to sit quietly, because most of us are just too action-oriented to feel comfortable taking such a break from a busy day. If you wait for some appropriate break in the midst of your day, not only will your earlier activities not benefit from your meditation, but also you'll be much more likely to skip meditation. So the first rule of thumb is to meditate first and then enjoy your day even more.

Meditate after Your Morning Shower or Bath

There are certainly exceptions to this rule, but most people feel fresher and more fully awake after their morning routine of brushing their teeth, bathing, and so on. Perhaps this is why for many centuries the tradition has existed in India to perform spiritual practices only after bathing in the morning. It's a wonderful feeling to be really fresh and then to close your eyes and dive deep within. You've cleansed your body; now you can cleanse your mind and spirit as well with the "mental bath" of meditation.

An exception to this might be if you wake up unusually early, say a couple of hours or more before you actually need to get up. Perhaps it is 3 or 4 AM, and you can't get back to sleep or don't feel the need to, or you simply have an urge to meditate. (Yes, it happens.) Then it's wonderful to just sit up in bed and meditate.

In the early-morning hours, or during the night, the world is still and silent. It's a perfect time to meditate for as long as you like, for an hour or even more if you don't fall back to sleep. Likely, though, you will eventually become sleepy; when you do, simply lie down and you will enjoy a deep, rejuvenating sleep, often with vivid dreams. The sleep that comes after an early-morning or nighttime meditation is especially healing and rejuvenating.

When I was living in a cave high in the Himalayas at the source of the Ganges River, I noticed that many of the holy men in that area seemed busy during the day — eating, doing laundry, collecting firewood, or just chatting among themselves while they sipped tea. I was spending every minute of my day meditating, and I began to wonder: weren't they also there to do spiritual practices? I finally asked and found that many of them meditated through much of each night. As one holy man told me, "That's the perfect time because the world is so still and silent; there are no thought forms in the atmosphere, so meditation is the most peaceful." It is also said that Saint Francis and other Christian mystics regularly meditated during the night.

You probably don't want to spend your nights in meditation, but if you do happen to wake up during the night or in the quiet hours of the early morning, rather than lie awake, why not use this time well? You'll be in good company. Otherwise, if you're a sound sleeper, a perfect time to meditate is right after bathing.

Meditate on an Empty Stomach

Meditation brings your entire mind and body into a state of deep rest, of stillness, of simply being. Your metabolic rate is lowered, whereas the process of digestion raises your metabolic rate. As a result, digestion and meditation conflict to some extent. To get the most out of your meditation, and to have the best digestion, it is better to meditate before a meal — before breakfast, for instance — rather than after. If you are so hungry that you can't sit still, perhaps have a light snack or a glass of water or juice before meditating to hold you over. If you have a full meal, ideally wait for a couple of hours before meditating. But if you are ever faced with the choice of meditating on a full stomach or not meditating at all, I'd meditate on a full stomach.

Meditate at the Same Point in Your Daily Routine

Making meditation a regular part of your daily routine will help immensely in establishing the habit of meditation. I advise making meditation as much a part of your morning routine as brushing your teeth. You don't wake up and wonder whether to brush your teeth, and you probably don't fret over whether you should brush them upon waking or perhaps wait until your lunch break at work. It's not even a question; you just brush your teeth. Ideally, meditation will become like this for you: a given, a part of your daily routine that sets you up to make the most of your day. Once your practice is established as a given, getting the benefits of meditation is also a given.

Meditate at Least Once a Day, and If You Can, Twice a Day

The morning meditation sets you up to get the most out of your day. You will likely find, though, that by the end of your workday some of the freshness, well-being, and clarity you felt after your morning meditation has faded. By the time you're done working, you may even feel like just going home and zoning out in front of the TV. Well, there's another option: take a second dive into the deep rest and relaxation of bliss consciousness.

You don't have to zone out in the evening. You can feel fresh, rested, and energized, capable of giving of yourself, whether to your family or to a creative project. Or you can simply more fully enjoy a relaxing evening. When I learned to meditate, I was taught to meditate twice a day, and that is what I have always done. If you are able to make this a part of your routine, the ideal time for your second meditation is sometime before dinner.

Even if you find that your evening meditation can't be as long as your morning meditation, better a shorter meditation in the evening than no meditation at all. If the needs of your family make it impossible to meditate once you step in the door, consider the possibility of a short meditation during a coffee break, or at the end of your workday, while still in your office. If your office isn't private, you could stop at a park on the way home and meditate on the grass under a tree. (It worked out well for the Buddha.) If the weather doesn't allow for that, you can sit in your car and meditate. I've done it many times. Or better yet, see if your family is interested in meditating with you at home. The point is, if gaining the benefits of meditation is important to you, you can find a way. And if you decide that once a day is simply more practical for you, that too is fine.

COMMIT TO IT!

Whatever meditation schedule you decide on, commit to it. Do it without fail. If such a commitment at first seems overwhelming, commit to sticking to your schedule without fail for just one month. After that month, well, commit for another month. After that, yes, another month. In other words, establishing the routine of daily meditation may at first require some discipline, but soon you will find that meditation is such an important, pleasant, and rewarding part of your day that it won't be a matter of commitment. You will look forward to those precious minutes of inner peace and bliss. They will become an indispensable part of your daily routine.

People looking on from the outside may think you have great self-discipline to meditate regularly, but you will know better: Does it take great discipline to eat a heaping bowl of your favorite ice cream twice a day? That's what meditation will become for you — you will savor it and won't want to miss it. It won't require discipline at all.

WHERE SHOULD YOU MEDITATE?

Where you meditate is really not so important. I've meditated in my bedroom and in my office; in planes, buses, and cars; in restaurants and the library; and in isolated caves — just about any place I've found myself when it was time to meditate.

It works wherever you are. It's ideal, of course, to meditate where you won't be disturbed, where you feel safe and secure turning your whole attention within, but if such a place is unavailable, you can meditate just about anywhere.

More often than not, you'll probably meditate at home. In that case, it's a good idea to have a spot dedicated to your meditation. If you can't have a dedicated meditation room, even a corner of your bedroom is fine. All you really need is a chair or cushion and, ideally, a place to lie down after meditating to come out slowly. I do suggest making your meditation place a comfortable and aesthetically pleasing spot that feels inviting to you, so that you'll look forward to sitting there. Even though your eyes are closed during meditation, it's uplifting to open your eyes to an appealing space as you finish.

Meditating in the same spot every day also has its benefits. As I mentioned earlier, meditation creates a vibratory influence in the atmosphere. This influence will build in a spot where you always meditate, and you will be able to feel it. Each time you sit there, the vibrations of that spot will draw you effortlessly into meditation, as well as have a soothing and healing effect on you. After a stressful day at work, that may be just what you need.

This is one reason caves have traditionally been considered ideal meditation spots (even though, as I discovered, they tend to be mighty cold). A cave becomes a cocoon of silence. You are protected from external influences while, day by day, the energy of your meditation builds. I'm not suggesting you dig a cave in your backyard (please don't), but you can make a corner of your bedroom your cave and build your own sacred vibrations there.

One final point about where to meditate: I'm often asked whether it's a good idea to meditate in nature. If you meditate in nature when you are first learning to meditate, the beauty and sounds around you may tend to draw your attention outward. For that reason, when you're first learning, you may find that you'll have deeper meditations if you meditate indoors. However, once you are familiar with diving within, meditating in nature can be an exquisite experience, and I highly recommend it. You will find that it develops a deep and satisfying sense of unity between you and your environment. As you transcend to finer, more expansive states within yourself, you will feel your oneness with all that surrounds you. It is like a glimpse of enlightenment. And opening your eyes to the beauty of nature is simply exquisite after diving deep within. I do recommend that you avoid meditating in direct sun, which is draining, though meditating in view of sunrise and sunset is wonderful.

So play it by ear. When the occasion arises to meditate in nature, by all means try it out. If you enjoy it, do it as often as you are moved to. At other times, enjoy meditating indoors at your own sacred meditation spot.

CHILDLIKE INNOCENCE

Years ago when I was traveling with Mata Amritanandamayi (Amma) and she addressed an audience, a student of meditation asked her, "I have been meditating for many years, yet I am not having any spiritual experience. I try and try, but nothing happens. What can I do?" Amma's answer revealed a secret of meditation: "Spiritual experience depends upon childlike innocence and faith."

Christ said that the kingdom of heaven is within you, and to enter the kingdom, you must be as innocent as a child. But what exactly does that mean? Well, watch children at play. One thing you may notice is that they spontaneously follow the charm of their experience. When they are having fun, they revel in it. If they become bored, they move on to more promising play. This is the essence of innocence — following our own intrinsic nature to seek more happiness. As we saw in chapter 1, this is also the key to successful meditation. Savor each moment of meditation; enjoy it with the quiet enthusiasm of a child at play. If you find yourself having thoughts, gently come back to the practice, which will take you toward inner bliss.

This raises another interesting point about childlike innocence: a child at play naturally expresses enthusiasm; he or she is not passive. You can go through the steps of meditation passively, without much care, or you can be fully alert, savoring every moment as if you were relishing your favorite dessert. Both approaches can be effortless, but there will be a world of difference in the results.

I call this quiet enthusiasm *creative receptivity*. Traditionally, people meditated in pursuit of the Divine, the Infinite, or liberation from suffering. They were highly motivated, vitally interested in the interior experience that meditation could provide (think of Saint Teresa of Avila or Rumi; you will not detect passivity in their writings). They meditated with childlike innocence and with an abundance of quiet enthusiasm, creative receptivity, or, you may simply say, love.

Creative receptivity is the attitude that you are ready to receive a gift, ready for something significant to happen. It's approaching meditation as if you're sitting on the edge of your chair, ready for the best. Perhaps you're ready at long last to feel relief from a constant, nagging anxiety or depression. Perhaps you're ready to embrace a more conscious, healthy lifestyle, to restore your cardiovascular health, or to enhance your artistic creativity or your sense of well-being. It may mean you're ready to dive deep into the bliss of your cosmic Self, or to explore what Saint Teresa of Avila called your interior mansion. You don't have to do anything to be creatively receptive. You need only *not* turn off and tune out.

Creative receptivity is one side of the innocence of a child at play. Another side is that a child innocently at play doesn't strain; the child's enjoyment is spontaneous. Many people I have talked to mistakenly think meditation is a matter of discipline — as if it's intrinsically a rather unpleasant task. Not so! Remember, meditation works *only* because it brings us to greater and greater happiness and eventually lands us in unrestricted joy, in bliss consciousness. As such, meditation is the essence of play.

So let yourself enjoy the play of your meditation. Enjoy every nuance. Be childlike and innocent in your inner, quiet play of meditation. Let it be spontaneous. Yes, there is structure to your meditation, but if you're having a delectable experience, let it lead you where it may; then come back to the steps of your meditation. Those steps are there only to be transcended. They are there to land you in unrestricted joy. And if you have a wonderful experience, be willing to let that go, too. Don't hold on to it. There are always bigger things yet to come. Spontaneity also means opening to all possibilities. In sum, meditation is the flow of grace that fulfills the heart and mind. You can't script grace. You can only receive and enjoy it, gratefully, with the innocence of a child.

A WORD ON CONCENTRATION

If you have taken other meditation classes, you may have heard a good deal of emphasis placed on something that is supposed to have a lot to do with meditation: concentration. To be honest, I don't like applying that word to meditation; it implies trying and effort, which is inimical to deep meditation because effort only agitates the mind.

Now that you've learned Effortless Mind meditation, you're ready to understand, based on your own experience, the actual role of concentration in meditation. It's not something you do; it's a state of absorption that occurs effortlessly when you have transcended to a subtle state. As you gain more clarity, you will discover that when you are in a very subtle state, steeped in blissful pure awareness, your attention naturally has laserlike power and focus. However, to arrive at such a subtle state, you must meditate with sublime ease; otherwise you will not transcend. Simply put: do not try to concentrate during meditation. Doing so will only agitate your mind to a more superficial level of experience. If you experience a state of concentration in meditation, it will happen easily. Concentration is not something you do, but is a state of experience to be achieved without effort.

HAND POSITIONING
DURING MEDITATION

In chapter 2 we briefly discussed posture and hand positioning during meditation. As I mentioned there, sitting erect but comfortably is the main consideration for optimizing your experience in meditation. However, adopting advanced postures, such as the lotus position, does have an effect energetically. For instance, when I first learned to sit in the lotus position for a length of time, I was amazed to find that assuming the position alone, without even meditating, seemed to awaken universal energy and consciousness.

Likewise, hand positioning can have a noticeably enhancing energetic effect. But while it may take months to gradually develop the ability to hold the lotus posture, there are traditional hand mudras that are easily learned and quite comfortable. Since students learning to meditate often express curiosity about hand placement, I'll describe a few classic hand mudras here. If one seems easy to you, and you feel a benefit in using it, by all means do use it.

First, what is a mudra? It is a gesture (often but not necessarily related to the hands) promoting a specific flow of prana; it also relates to a particular attitude, emotionally, mentally, and spiritually. Meditators frequently report that adopting a hand mudra deepens their experience and seems to connect them with cosmic energies. A few hand mudras you may use during meditation:

- BHAIRAVA MUDRA. Place your hands in your lap, palms up, right over left. Bhairava is a particularly fearsome aspect of Shiva, who is not only pure consciousness but also the divine force of destruction. Why does such a peaceful-looking hand placement have such a fierce appellation? Because Shiva is transcendental consciousness, ever at peace, and his work of dissolution in its highest form consists of drawing the universe back into its source — that universal consciousness prior to creation where there is only perfect peace.

- CHIN MUDRA. First, join the tip of your index finger with the tip of your thumb while keeping your middle, ring, and little fingers comfortably extended (they needn't be perfectly straight) and slightly apart. Alternately, instead of joining the tip of the index finger and thumb, you can either place the first joint of the index finger under the first joint of the thumb, or place the tip of the index finger at the root of the thumb. This may make it easier for you to hold the position for the entire meditation.

  Chin refers to consciousness, so this mudra is the gesture of pure consciousness. The index finger represents your individual consciousness and the thumb represents universal consciousness; their union suggests that individual consciousness is united with universal consciousness. The three extended fingers represent the three *gunas*, or essential constituents of nature. The fingers are extended — that is, nature is out of the picture; you have transcended the world.

  To complete the mudra, place your hands on your knees, with your palms up, toward the unbounded sky, representative of your unbounded consciousness. Placing the hands on the knees is also significant. It activates prana to flow through a nadi that runs from the knees up the inside of the thighs to the perineum, the site of the root chakra. This in turn helps to activate and open the root chakra.

Remember my description of my first experience of the chakras while I slept? I was surprised at the time that the experience distinctly began with a rush of energy from my inner thighs into my root chakra. This didn't make any sense to me, even when I later learned about the chakras, which start in the perineum and go up from there. What was the reason for the distinct sensation of energy in my inner thighs that immediately prefaced my experience of the chakras? Only many years later did I learn of this particular nadi, which is called *gupta nadi*, or the hidden nadi. Energy flowing through this nadi, which runs up the inner thighs into the root chakra, is well known by yogis as a stimulus for the opening of the root chakra and for sending energy up the nadis in and around the spine to open the other chakras. The mystery was solved.

- JNANA MUDRA. This gesture is exactly like the chin mudra, only your hands are placed palms down on your knees. *Jnana* means "knowledge." Knowledge is very closely related to consciousness, but knowledge ordinarily entails a subject and an object. In the chin mudra, the hands face upward, representing complete transcendence. In the jnana mudra, the hands face downward, indicating some relationship of pure consciousness with the world, but the finger placement also indicates complete transcendence. What

can be the significance, then? When pure consciousness relates to the world, the result is revelation. The
highest revelation is absolute knowledge — that is,
the recognition that all is one's own Self. This is the
highest level of knowledge, where the duality between
knower and known dissolves into a grand unity. This
is the meaning of the jnana mudra.

There you have it. Each mudra is said to stimulate the
emotional, mental, and spiritual state that it represents. If it is
comfortable for you to adopt one of these mudras during meditation, try it for a few meditations and see what you notice.

WHAT YOU PUT
INTO YOUR BODY MATTERS

Although meditation is independent of any particular lifestyle
or diet, I would be remiss if I did not point out that what you
put into your body will make a difference in the quality of
your meditation and how quickly you advance in your inner
experience. Smoking, for instance, in addition to its effects on
physical health, makes the prana crude, blocks the nadis, and
dulls the mind. The use of alcoholic drinks and recreational
drugs similarly dulls the mind and senses, creating biochemical imbalances as well as clogging the nadis. These are not
moral judgments, but rather conclusions based on the direct
experience of many. If you wish to confirm this for yourself,
simply abstain from these substances for a few months while
meditating regularly (which develops your subtle perception), and then try them again. You will see for yourself their

effects. In fact, this is how the qualities of various foods and substances have been discerned by yogis throughout the centuries: through direct experience.

As this suggests, diet is a consideration when it comes to meditation. I am not a nutritional expert and do not make dietary recommendations, but I have noticed a few things about the effects of food on meditation, and many of these observations are in line with the observations of yogis over the centuries. I'll mention just a few basics, many of which may be obvious to you already:

- A diet high in fresh (preferably organic) fruits and vegetables is especially conducive to clarity of mind at the subtle levels.
- Foods that are heavy and harder to digest, like red meat, tend to have a dulling effect on meditation and block the nadis.
- Overeating is dulling.
- Avoid foods that you are sensitive or allergic to; consistently eating such foods will put your body out of balance. (There are tests that can reveal hidden food allergies that might be affecting your energy level, mood, health, and skin without your even knowing. For more information, see the Resources section.)
- Appropriate Ayurvedic herbs (Ayurveda is the ancient traditional medicine of India) of a pure quality can help balance and strengthen your body and result in deeper, clearer meditations.
- Avoid cooking with a microwave, and also avoid overcooking. The method of food preparation affects the

vibrational quality of your food. Using a microwave oven to cook, as well as overcooking by other means, depletes the prana in your food.

- Avoid foods that have been genetically modified and dairy products from cows treated with hormones.

In the discussion of the chin mudra, I mentioned the three gunas. This is a concept of the Samkhya system of Indian philosophy and provides a deeper understanding of the effects of foods and other substances. Essentially, all of nature is comprised of the three gunas — *rajas*, *tamas*, and *sattva* — each of which has particular attributes. Rajas is the impulse toward action and movement; tamas is a retarding force; sattva is the force of balance and harmony. The interaction of these three accounts for all change, growth, and evolution in nature. The influence of these three is also present, in varying degrees, in everything in existence, including everything we eat:

- Foods dominated by the quality of rajas, the principle of activity, are stimulating. Such foods include hot spices and stimulants like coffee and caffeinated tea. Generally, such foods are not ideal for meditation because they increase restlessness in the mind.

- Foods dominated by the quality of tamas, the principle of inertia and negation, increase dullness and lethargy. Such foods include alcoholic drinks, red meat, eggs, mushrooms, fried foods, and food that is no longer fresh. Again, such foods are less than ideal for meditation due to their dulling effect.

- Foods dominated by the quality of sattva, the principle of balance, harmony, and purity, increase clarity, contentment, and well-being. Such foods include most fresh vegetables (not the nightshades or spicy or pungent vegetables, such as hot peppers and onions), legumes, mild spices, properly prepared nuts (for instance, soaked and blanched almonds), and many herbs. As you might expect, a diet high in these foods is ideal to promote clarity in your meditation.

This, admittedly, offers just a glimpse of the application of the concept of the three gunas to meditation. You will benefit from meditation no matter what your diet or lifestyle, but as in anything, we can also learn much from those who came before us.

Following these dietary principles not only will accelerate your progress through meditation but also can profoundly improve your health. About a year ago, I was diagnosed with Hashimoto's disease, a disorder in which the immune system attacks your thyroid. This is a serious condition, and in Western medicine there is no cure for it; it is treated by thyroid hormone replacement, usually for life (while the thyroid dies).

How I got this was a mystery to me, since I thought I was eating and living well, getting adequate exercise, and so on. I may never know the complete answer, which probably involves a number of factors, like genetics and environmental toxins as well as diet. The good news: not only did I not have to go on thyroid replacement hormones, but also my most recent tests show that my autoimmunity has been reversed; there is no sign of Hashimoto's in my system. My thyroid is fine.

How did this happen? Through a combination of Ayurvedic assessment and functional-medicine testing, I found out which foods were causing my immune system to react to my thyroid. I followed the diet that was right for me (this is individual, determined by various constitutional factors), which consisted of organic fruits and vegetables, plant proteins, and natural supplements prescribed for me.

This may seem to have little to do with meditation, but your health is important, and it can profoundly affect your ability to meditate. Anytime your body is inflamed and reactive, so is your mind. In fact, this is precisely why Ayurveda, the ancient traditional medicine of India, developed as a sister science to Yoga — to keep your body healthy and balanced in order to support your personal growth.

If you are interested in learning more about dietary considerations and Ayurveda, see the Resources section.

CHAPTER 9

MEDITATION
The Purifying Fire

How does a person grow? We have already seen that your inmost Self is infinite; in fact, your essence is the source of all love, of all joy, of all creative intelligence. So what is holding you back from expressing your full potential? The detailed answer to this question is complex, but the science of Yoga provides a simple general answer: something must be blocking the inner light of the Self from shining through in its full glory. Remove that blockage and your true inner light will shine.

This is an important principle. It means you do not have to bring something new to yourself to somehow *develop* your full potential. In fact, it means you cannot be the *cause* of your full potential. Your full potential is already present within you. To live your full potential, you need only remove the blockages. This process of removal is called purification. As we shall see, this is what meditation is all about.

Purification can take place on many levels; in fact, it takes place on all the levels of your being, within all the koshas (the sheaths). For instance, within the physical sheath (the physical body), biochemical imbalances are normalized for optimal health and balance; on the level of the energetic sheath, the obstructions in the nadis are melted to allow the even and balanced flow of prana (for optimal health and balance, as well as for higher consciousness). On the level of the mental/emotional sheath, attachments, aversions, fear, and so on are released. On the level of the intellect/wisdom sheath, ignorance of the true nature of things and identification with the ego are dissolved. You may learn various skills and accomplish a great deal in your outer life, but only a profound process of inner purification will allow you to realize your true Self and enjoy life fully. That is the process of meditation.

You might well wonder where the blocks, imbalances, and impurities come from. Simply, they are the residual impressions of past experience — stress, trauma, excess or imbalance in lifestyle, maladaptive patterns in relating to the world, and so on. All these leave their mark on the various levels of your being. As we have already seen, all of the layers of your being are profoundly interrelated, and so are the blockages. For instance, a pattern of fear in your life will have a physical, biochemical basis, which will also correlate with blockages in your nadis. This is why, for instance, for complete healing a holistic medical practice requires addressing not just the physical manifestations of a problem but the mind as well.

So what do you need to know about purification? The first thing to know is that in order to receive the benefits of meditation, purification must take place. That's just the nature of the process. It's also important to understand how purification will show itself in your meditation, so that you'll know how to handle various experiences. Without this understanding, confusion can arise, and you might think you're doing something wrong. So let us look at this process by which you will gradually live more and more of your full potential.

THE MIRACLE OF SLEEP

You may not have realized it, but you have already been regularly practicing a miraculously efficient process of purification, every night in fact. You go to bed after a full day, feeling tired, perhaps barely able to keep your eyes open, and you fall asleep, only to wake up some seven or eight hours later feeling fresh and ready for another day. This restoration of your body and mind through sleep is miraculous. Think of it: were it not for sleep, what would be the quality of your life? How do you feel after missing even a single night's sleep? This miracle of sleep is essential to your well-being and ultimately to life itself.

Scientists do not understand everything about sleep, but they do know that during sleep the body undergoes many important changes. Neurotoxins are neutralized, tissues are repaired and regenerated, growth hormones are released, bones and muscles grow, and the immune system is strengthened. The restfulness of sleep is essential to health in many ways. So what does this have to do with meditation?

Meditation, too, provides the body with rest and relaxation, though of a different quality; you are deeply rested and relaxed in meditation but also fully aware. Just as sleep heals and restores your body, so does meditation, though in unique ways. Perhaps you have already noticed that when you meditate, not only do you feel deeply and pleasantly relaxed, but also your breathing becomes very faint, indicating a state of metabolic rest. In fact, meditation creates a response that is essentially the opposite of the fight-or-flight response, and research has also shown that meditation reduces stress hormones (adrenaline, noradrenaline, and cortisol).

What is the benefit of this? You may by now be able to answer that from your own experience. Have you noticed that after meditating you generally feel more relaxed and calm yet also more alert and energized? This is the effect of the physiological changes that take place during meditation, just as feeling refreshed and ready for another day is the effect of a good night's sleep.

Now, notice that both sleep and meditation consist of cycles of differing states and experiences. During a typical night's sleep, you cycle through several stages of nonrapid eye movement (NREM) sleep and rapid eye movement (REM) sleep. Most, but not all, of your dreams occur during REM sleep. In meditation you also experience cycles: you may have periods of deep inner silence and expanded awareness, perhaps accompanied by the awareness of energy in the body; other periods where there is little sense of expanded awareness but plenty of daydreams or mundane thoughts; and still other periods where deep silence and expanded awareness are accompanied by peripheral thoughts. Sound familiar?

Often, thoughts spontaneously arise and may even seem to take you "away" from your meditation. You're not deliberately thinking these thoughts; they're simply happening. But why are they happening? Recall the natural attraction of the mind toward pure happiness: Why isn't the mind drawn only inward by the lure of increasing happiness as it experiences the charm of the inner peace, stillness, and expansiveness that lie within? What is it that works against this fundamental force of gravity pulling your mind within?

Maharishi Mahesh Yogi offered a brilliant answer to this question. He proposed that the involuntary thoughts you experience in meditation — whether mundane to-do lists, memories of conversations with others, daydreams, or thoughts about the meditation itself — are the mental side effect of biochemical processes that are taking place to restore and rejuvenate your body. In other words, the thoughts are the mental smoke arising from the biological processes, the "fire of purification," initiated by the mind's journey within.

The cycles in your meditation — from inner silence to active thinking — are entirely natural, just as natural as the cycles during a night's sleep. And thoughts are *not* happening because you are doing anything wrong. In fact, these cycles, in both sleep and meditation, are the very means by which your body and mind are restored, normalized, and purified. This leads us to a remarkable conclusion: experiencing uninvited thoughts during meditation is an essential part of successful meditation.

To better understand this, recall the intimate relationship between mind and body that you experience during meditation. As the mind comes to subtler states of experience, the body's functioning changes and a myriad of measurable physiological changes take place that indicate deep physiological rest, relaxation, and reduction of stress. In other words, your mind profoundly affects the functioning of your body.

But it works both ways. As the body undergoes the complex processes of biological purification during meditation, something must change in the mind, given the intimate relationship between mind and body. Many of the thoughts you experience in meditation are the result of this process.

If this seems like only a theory to you, you may verify it for yourself, just as the yogis and contemplatives have done for centuries, by intensifying your experience of meditation. You can do this by going on a retreat where you meditate many hours a day. Almost surely you will experience not only deeper and clearer meditations but also periods where the number, frequency, and intensity of thoughts are far greater than when meditating once or twice a day at home. Many times I have heard meditators on retreat say their minds were practically boiling with thoughts. The greater the depth of the meditation cycle, the more intense the purification cycle.

Hopefully this will eliminate any doubt for you about thoughts being a natural part of your meditation. They are the unavoidable mental consequence of a physiological process of purification. They are entirely natural, a necessary part of the meditation because, in a very significant sense, meditation is *for* purification. Only by purifying your mind-body complex will you enjoy more clarity, creativity, peace, and well-being after meditating. Only by purifying yourself will you gradually begin to live higher consciousness and become established in your higher Self. When it comes to unfolding your full creative and spiritual potential, purification is in large part the name of the game.

This means there is no need to feel bad about thoughts in meditation at all, any more than you would feel bad about having dreams during sleep. Dreams during a night's sleep serve the necessary purpose of normalizing brain chemistry. So too do thoughts in meditation. If you have a meditation that is absolutely roiling with thoughts, congratulate yourself: profound and positive changes are taking place within you. Again, *all* the cycles of meditation work in concert to restore your body to true normalcy, balance, and health.

This doesn't mean you should *try* to have thoughts in meditation or look at meditation as your chance to daydream, reflect on a recently seen movie, or create to-do lists. I'm speaking of thoughts as they arise naturally in the course of practicing the techniques of meditation as I've described them. Simply continue with your meditation without minding the thoughts.

Having understood the process of purification, you are now in a position to understand why there is no useful purpose in judging your meditation. Naturally, when you have a deep, clear, blissful meditation, you may feel gratified. Yet that depth and clarity is only setting the platform for further purification, and when that purification starts, you're bound to have more thoughts. But this will result in deeper, clearer meditations later. So it's all good. It's all natural. The best thing you can do is to simply allow nature to take its course.

MANAGING THE PURIFICATION PROCESS

Managing the purification process during meditation is, for the most part, very simple: you need only understand that thoughts, the most common expression of purification, are a natural part of the meditation. Let them go, continue meditating without minding them, and voilà! The process of purification is managed and will go on automatically. The key is to neither purposely engage in thoughts nor resist them. If you become engaged in thoughts unintentionally, that's fine. When you realize it, just gently return to your practice.

But let's say that at some point during a meditation you find you are absorbed in thinking about what you have to do that day. You didn't sit down with the intention to plan your day; you sat down in good faith to meditate. Yet you became engrossed in thoughts. This unconscious engrossment is simply the mental result of purification. You are still meditating correctly.

Once you become aware that you are planning your day, you have the opportunity to continue with the steps of meditation — for instance, to move on to the next chakra. If, however, you consciously decide to continue to plan out your day, then at that point you are no longer meditating. There is a world of difference between being innocently absorbed in thoughts during the process of meditating and *choosing* to contemplate something other than the object of meditation during meditation. The former is a part of meditation, even if you're innocently absorbed in sundry thoughts for twenty minutes straight; the latter is something else, even if it lasts only two minutes. It is absolutely fine to have thoughts in meditation, but once you realize you've been thinking and you have a choice, that is the time to return to your practice.

To resist thoughts is another way to depart from the practice of meditation; it violates the first essential principle of meditating with sublime ease. Let's say that you have heard you should not have thoughts in meditation, that meditation means sitting in inner stillness. In fact, many people come to my classes with this idea. Once they close their eyes and discover they are beset with all manner of thoughts, they try to push their thoughts away. But it is entirely useless to engage in a wrestling match with thoughts. No one can quiet thoughts through control; the more you try, the more unruly your mind will become.

Remember, nature is doing the meditation, not you. You transcend only because of the innate tendency of the mind to be drawn toward the peace and bliss of pure awareness. This is beyond your control; you can't make yourself transcend. Likewise, the sundry thoughts occurring during meditation are the result of physiological purification. In either case, the laws of nature are conducting the meditation. Fight it, pit yourself against the nature of your mind and body, and you will certainly lose. Fighting nature will *create* stress instead of dissolving it. Again, just gently come back to the practice of meditation without fighting anything.

Other experiences, besides thoughts, may arise in meditation as a result of purification. Let's look briefly at some of these.

Images, Colors, and Mystical Experiences

People often see imagery or colors during meditation. The advice I've given for thoughts applies to visual experiences too: don't mind the images or colors; neither engage nor resist, just continue to meditate. Such experiences are typically by-products of the purification process.

If, however, you have an experience that is profoundly compelling, such as a sublime experience of bliss that comes with the inner perception of color, this may or may not be the by-product of purification; it could be a clear, subtle perception. For instance, you could experience the lotuslike form of the chakras, a blissful, golden inner light, or a glimpse of a higher being. If you have such an experience that you know in your heart is a subtle perception, by all means enjoy it. When it becomes less compelling, continue with your meditation.

The number and flavors of possible experiences in meditation are unlimited. The entire universe is within you and may be experienced in meditation. Consider the writings of the great mystics who have recorded some of their experiences — Rumi, Saint Teresa of Avila, William Blake, Saint John of the Cross — as well as yogis, like the author of the Yoga Sutras, Patanjali. How many flavors of divine bliss and ecstasy can you experience in meditation — how much love, compassion, devotion; how many visions of celestial realms or flights into the heights of heaven? These cannot all be dismissed as purification. Yet it's not to your advantage to follow every flight and fancy that might come during meditation. That could take you on any number of tangents and your progress would suffer.

The primary objective of meditation is not to have a flashy experience but to unfold your consciousness and develop your heart and mind in order to express all the joy, love, and creative intelligence you can in your life. Enlightenment may dawn, too, but enlightenment itself is not a flashy experience; it is true normalcy, living all you are, to your fullest creative and spiritual potential, every day, with an innocent heart and mind fully opened. On your path, flashy experiences will come for sure, and they will also go. Simple, pure being — your innermost, infinite Self — remains eternally.

So when it comes to mystical experiences in meditation, the safest course is to treat them like any other thought and come back to the practice. As has been noted by many teachers, including Patanjali, enlightenment will not dawn in someone attached to flashy experiences, spiritual knowledge, psychic abilities, or bliss, any more than it will dawn in one attached to the body and pleasures of the senses. Enlightenment embraces the wholeness of life, and to rise to that state, a person gradually ceases to judge one thing as better than another and instead expands beyond such dualities. In the words of the great Chinese sage Sengtsan:

> *If you wish to know the truth,*
> *then hold to no opinions for or against anything.*
> *To set up what you like against what you dislike*
> *is the disease of the mind.*

Physical Expressions of Purification

Now and then while meditating you may feel physical sensations of heat, cold, or tingling. Perhaps your torso or limbs feel very heavy or light. This is entirely normal. It is either the result of biochemical purification or the flow of prana through the nadis, or both. It need not distract you from your meditation; notice the sensations and then continue.

At some point on your path as a meditator, you may find that you physically feel so light that it seems you might float away or even shoot into the sky. This is the result of spiritual energy awakening and is often accompanied by great bliss. Just enjoy it if it seems compelling, and then continue your meditation. And don't worry: you are in no danger of actually taking off, even though it might seem so.

Sometimes purification may result in physical movement, perhaps a gentle rocking motion or even a more pronounced movement, such as your head moving or your body adopting certain positions. This is relatively rare, but nothing to be concerned about if it happens. Just continue meditating without minding it. If the movement becomes distracting, you can open your eyes until it stops, and then close your eyes and continue to meditate. Don't encourage the movement, but also don't forcibly resist it. Just don't give it much attention.

What causes such movement? If the prana is awakened while there are obstructions in the nadis, the body may move to facilitate the flow through the blockages. It is like turning on the garden hose when the hose has some bends or kinks in it: it may move around a bit. Such movements may continue for some time, but eventually they will stop when the blockages in the nadis are clear.

Emotional and Mental Expressions of Purification

On rare occasions of intense purification, you may feel somewhat spacey, emotional, irritable, or distracted after meditation. This can be due to purification carrying over into activity, but most likely it is a result of coming out of meditation too rapidly. Always spend at least three to five minutes lying in the corpse pose to come out of meditation and smoothly transition into activity. If this doesn't help, and you are indeed going through purification so intense that the purification continues even after you come out of meditation, there are several things you can do:

- Stay in the corpse pose for longer than five minutes, until you feel more settled.
- Shorten your meditation time. For instance, if you're meditating thirty minutes, meditate twenty instead to slow the pace of purification.
- Practice gentle breathing exercises to soothe and balance your system. On my website, I offer video instruction in a number of such techniques, such as the alternating nostril pranayama. These are wonderful adjuncts to meditation that will not only deepen your experience and accelerate your progress but also help ensure that your progress is smooth and comfortable.
- Practice gentle, soothing forms of *yogasanas* (yoga postures). Note that more rigorous routines of yoga may stir up more purification, so if you're doing yoga to soothe yourself, be gentle and easy. This will balance the energies in your body as well as your emotions.
- Engage in physical exercise, especially in nature, such as a vigorous walk, hike, or bicycle ride.
- Dynamically engage in your daily routine. Do not just sit around all day waiting for the inner clouds to clear. Likely they won't clear until you do fully engage yourself in your daily life.

With Effortless Mind meditation, it is rare for someone to experience any discomfort due to purification, but if you do, these measures should help keep you comfortable and on track. If symptoms continue, please see a licensed medical professional.

Though purification is usually comfortable, going on almost unnoticed and only during the meditation itself, it is a fact both of spiritual life and of natural healing processes. When holistic health practitioners talk of a "healing crisis," essentially they are referring to a process of purification. Understanding and accepting the realities of purification are essential to staying on any spiritual or natural healing path, and it is important that spiritual teachers and guides address the issue. The all-time expert on the subject is no doubt Saint John of the Cross, who in *Dark Night of the Soul* and *Ascent of Mount Carmel* wrote extensively about purification to reassure his spiritual charges. In any case, a true spiritual seeker will not demand only bliss from life. Embrace all of life, just as it is, with its inevitable peaks and valleys. That is the way to wholeness.

NOISE IN MEDITATION

Our world is not a silent place. At one time or another you are almost sure to be faced with noise that threatens to interrupt the peace of your meditation. Traffic noise, voices, doors closing, music, neighbors blowing leaves, lawnmowers, power saws — all these and more are inevitable and nearly ubiquitous sounds of modern life. What to do? Build a soundproof meditation room? The good news is there's no need. Noise needn't interfere with your meditation one bit.

You may have already noticed that sometimes during

meditation you're aware of noise, possibly even bothered by it; and at other times, though you know there are sounds in the environment — perhaps even the same sounds that on other occasions have disturbed you — you hardly notice them. This is a very common experience. What makes for this difference? The difference lies within the experiencer, within you.

What is awareness of noise during meditation? It is nothing more or less than a thought, and as we've seen, thoughts arise from purification. In other words, when noise becomes an issue for you in meditation, it is probably because you're going through a cycle of purification and your mind finds the noise a convenient focal point, so you begin to think about it.

For example, let's say you're meditating while a motorcycle goes by. You may or may not notice the sound. If you don't, there will be no question of being disturbed by the sound. But what if you do notice the sound? What if the sound grabs your attention and elicits thoughts? Well, actually it's not the sound that's the issue; it's only the thought about the sound that is the issue. So, how do we treat thoughts in meditation? Exactly: we just don't mind them. Let them go as they come, and gently return to your practice.

That's it. With that simple attitude, you have sound-proofed your meditation. You can strive to silence your environment as much as you like — tell the kids to be quiet, give your dog a bone, ask your neighbors to stop mowing. You can drive yourself crazy trying to create complete silence, and yet the birds will still sing, there will be traffic, and people will talk and play music. You might as well accept it. It's not about creating silence. It's about how to be in relationship with the thoughts you are having: simply, gently return to your practice. As you do, you'll find the sound gradually retreats from your awareness, and you'll likely go through many minutes of meditation without even noticing it. If again you notice the sound, simply return to your practice.

To share a personal story: I learned how to deal with noise the hard way while I was attending an extended meditation retreat in the early 1970s. This course, which lasted six months, was held at a vacation resort on the southern coast of Spain during the off-season. The off-season in Spain, it turns out, is the perfect time for building newer and bigger resorts, which is exactly what was happening — just outside my window.

So as I sat meditating nearly all of every day, month after month, not only did I endure the usual sounds of construction — hammering, cranes, yelling, jackhammers — but even the pounding of a huge pile driver right outside my window. With each booming crash of the pile driver, every forty-five seconds or so, my entire apartment would shake. As you might imagine, at first all this nearly drove me crazy, but I soon learned that I could meditate undisturbed even by this. In fact, this was excellent training, for after the course was over and I returned to college, I discovered that my new roommate loved to play hard rock cranked to the max while I meditated on my bunk....

SLEEP IN MEDITATION

You may have heard that you should never fall asleep in meditation, and that if you do, your teacher is liable to sneak up and whack you on the head with a stick, right? (That's one advantage to learning through this book; I'm not there to whack you.) Actually, in almost forty years of teaching, I have yet to whack any student with a stick for any reason, but I definitely would not do it to wake someone up. As long as you're entering meditation with sincerity and not looking at it as a chance to grab a quick nap, as long as you're meditating with creative receptivity and not passivity, falling asleep almost surely means you need the kind of rest that sleep provides. In other words, it is just as natural as having thoughts, for it is part of the process of purification through meditation. It means that because of the restfulness of meditation, fatigue is dissolving and being released; the result is drowsiness or even sleep. It's okay. It's even a good thing.

For several years, I taught meditation at a popular ashram in southern India. There I met a number of people who subscribed to the notion that you simply mustn't fall asleep in meditation. They were very dedicated to their spiritual growth and often stayed up late either doing service work or spending time with their spiritual teacher (Amma, who famously seems to get by on only a couple of hours of sleep a night, if that). As a result, these dedicated seekers were often tired, and when they sat to meditate, they felt sleepy. Yet they forced themselves to stay awake. They made meditation a battleground against their fatigue, and so meditation became for them not an experience of bliss consciousness but of frustration. Not surprisingly, such individuals may quit meditating altogether. They may feel they cannot do it. Indeed, they cannot meditate successfully as long as they insist on breaking the first essential principle of meditation: sublime ease.

I believe it is far better to adopt the attitude of Saint Therese of Lisieux when it comes to sleep in meditation. Saint Therese, a cloistered Carmelite nun, often dozed during her hours of prayer. After seven years of battling this tendency, she finally accepted what was happening to her: "I remember," she writes in her autobiography, "that little children are as pleasing to their parents when they are asleep as well as when they are wide awake; I remember, too, that when they perform operations, doctors put their patients to sleep."

Indeed, the sleep that comes during meditation can be profoundly healing and rejuvenating. Saint Therese of Lisieux was correct: the Divine *is* performing an operation on you. Many times over the years, I have been struck by how deep and powerful meditation seemed after waking up following an involuntary snooze. So if you ever find yourself falling asleep in meditation, simply lean against something to provide back support. If you do start to nod off, don't fight it. When you wake up, complete your meditation. Miracles can happen while you're asleep during meditation; accept this gift with gratitude.

CHAPTER 10

MAKING LIFE
A MEDITATION

Why do you meditate? This may seem a simple question, but it is one worth considering. For some the answer might be easy: "I want to learn to relax," "I'm meditating so I can sleep better," "I want to get rid of the anxiety I feel," or "I want to be happier." You may have another answer to this question. You may meditate for health reasons, to learn to better manage stress, or to develop your creativity. All these and many other reasons are perfectly valid, and there's excellent cause to believe that, with regular practice, meditation will fulfill your desire. If these are all you're seeking from meditation, then you need read no further. You have what you need. Just practice as you've been taught in this book, once or preferably twice a day, and live your life as consciously and sensibly as you can. If you do, there is every chance you will begin to enjoy the benefits you wish for and more.

There is, however, another possible reason to meditate.

Meditation is, after all, a spiritual practice, one that, in some form or another, has roots in the heart of most, if not all, of the world's great spiritual traditions. Traditionally, the purpose of meditation has been to bring seekers to a state of union with the Divine. If a deepened spiritual connection or profound personal transformation is your goal for meditating — or a goal for your life — read on.

IT'S ALL ABOUT INTEGRATION

When I first started to meditate as a teenager, all I sought was to know God. I couldn't have cared less about any of the other benefits of meditation. I had read various Eastern scriptures and had a burning desire to merge into the Divine. Eventually, after years of dedicated practice, I did gain the inner clarity to experience the Divine during meditation. Throughout history, countless mystics have experienced the Divine regularly during their spiritual practices. It is not such a far-off goal if you are deeply motivated. Meditation is remarkably effective as a tool to make the mind subtle enough to experience the Divine — during meditation, that is. However, eventually I realized that my real goal — enlightenment, union with the Divine 24/7 — was eluding me.

Experiencing the Divine during meditation is wonderful, but experiences, however wonderful, come and go. They pass. If the sublime experiences during meditation do not translate into higher consciousness when your eyes are open and a transformed quality of action during the day, then something's amiss. The divine consciousness and feeling you experience in meditation are not being integrated; they're failing to purify and transform the relative aspects of your being — your mind, heart, personality, and ego. Meditation is easy. The real challenge is to integrate what you experience in meditation, so that the grace you feel in meditation breathes through every moment of your day. This is the true path to enlightenment, one that requires more than meditating with eyes closed. It requires, in a sense, making every moment of your day a meditation.

MEDITATE AND ACT

My first teacher taught that to gain enlightenment, all that is needed is to "meditate [twice daily] and act." There is considerable wisdom in this. First, it is important to meditate. Connecting daily with your higher Self is essential to help keep your life in a flow of personal growth. Yet action, too, is essential. It will not serve you to retire to a cave and meditate all day long, day in and day out. You need other activities to integrate the effects of meditation into the mind, heart, and personality. All the demands of daily life — relationships, work, school, and so on — encourage you to actualize your potential, to expand and deepen your personality, heart, and mind.

For this reason, just as my first teacher taught, full engagement in action following meditation is a good starting point to serve the goal of integration. It will help ground you, increase your confidence, and strengthen your sense of self, as well as lead to success that may help provide you with a sense of security in the world. Focused, dynamic action is also important in moving the life force awakened during meditation through the subtle channels (the nadis) in your body. Halfhearted or lazy action is ineffective and weakening. Not only will it fail to meet with success, but also it won't move the life force through your body. Your energies will lie fallow and the nadis will stay blocked, and this will retard your progress. Connecting with your infinite Self by meditating and then neglecting to act and interact with others is like eating a rich, nutritious meal and then lounging all day on the couch. That nutritious potential just turns into fat.

Unfortunately, the statement "meditate and act" was often interpreted to mean that you could meditate and then simply act just as you always had and an enlightened state of life would soon dawn. Nothing could be further from the truth. If you continue to act as you always have — even if you *fully* engage in acting dynamically — you will enjoy some of the benefits of meditating, but you won't integrate higher consciousness into your life to a significant degree. You may well feel more relaxed, lighter, healthier, happier, clearer, and more creative, but your ego will remain fully intact. Any degree of actual enlightenment will elude you. Indeed, the bliss you feel in meditation may even feed your ego.

Let me give you a personal example of this and how failing to understand the need for integration can wreak havoc in your life, producing results opposite of what you would expect from meditation.

My relationship with my brother-in-law had always been a cordial one until one day when this mysteriously changed. Suddenly, at every family gathering, he was blatantly rude to me. All my extended family noticed it, but no one could figure out the reason for his behavior. Many members of the family spoke to him about it, but he wouldn't change his attitude or reveal what was bothering him. I asked him and got the brick-wall treatment. I asked my sister, and she claimed not to know. This went on for years, until finally the answer came out.

In the early 1990s, I had not yet really understood the principle of integration. In fact, it seemed to me the more I meditated, the better. I often took days of silence, during which I would fast and meditate all day. Well, one day my brother-in-law had asked me to help him build a ramp at the family vacation home for his wife, my sister, who is wheelchair-bound. I had turned him down because I was planning to spend the day in meditation. This was the event that had upset him. I am embarrassed now to say that it didn't occur to me then that this act of service might have been far more important than my private retreat. How could I have been so insensitive and self-centered?

When I found out that this was what had upset my brother-in-law, I was mortified. I called him, apologized profusely, and asked his forgiveness. I told him I completely understood his feelings and only wished I had known sooner. Finally, the mystery was solved and our relationship returned to one of friendship and mutual appreciation. It was a huge lesson for me on the value of integration.

For better or worse, most human beings are by default considerably self-centered and unconscious in their behavior. Unfortunately, meditating, in itself, doesn't change this. So much of our behavior each day is determined not by conscious choice but by subconscious, often self-defeating, patterns established in our childhood. How could remaining this way ever assist you in achieving enlightenment? Acting as you always have, no matter how much or how well you meditate, will not transform you into a loving, selfless human being.

To grow toward enlightenment, you must consciously transform how you place your attention in the world in order to purify your motivations and refine the qualities of your heart and mind. Your behavior need not be determined simply by patterns established in childhood. Your actions, your life, can become conscious, mindful, and loving. When the pure awareness you experience in meditation is applied to living mindfully, it will result in countless instances of new awareness (transformative insights) that will enable you to act with greater empathy, compassion, openness, gratitude, and grace. This is the path tread by seekers of perfection in all the world's great spiritual traditions throughout the centuries.

MINDFULNESS AND THE POWER OF ATTENTION

Mindfulness is an essential key to integrating the benefits of meditation. You may have heard the term defined in many ways: as maintaining present-moment awareness; nonjudgmentally accepting thoughts, feelings, and sensations as they are; being mindful of your breath as a meditation or as a centering technique during activity; maintaining a calm awareness of your thoughts and feelings; and so on. All of these are valuable practices and in fact closely relate to the way I use the term.

By *mindfulness*, I mean maintaining a calm inner awareness of your thoughts and feelings, but especially when you are under stress, when you react in some way. Further, it is an awareness of not only thoughts and feelings but also the more subtle habitual patterns of attention and subconscious beliefs that underlie and give rise to the thoughts and feelings that tend to limit you. Let me give an example.

Not long ago, a friend of mine revealed he had often suffered from depression and sadness in his life. He was a spiritually minded person who had done some meditation and had practiced mindfulness, but he told me that no amount of non-judgmentally witnessing his sadness had ever really helped, at least as far as he could tell. His sadness and depression had persisted. Then one day he had a revelation. He became aware of the pattern of attention underlying his frequent sadness. He realized he was always looking for what was missing in his life. His mind did this automatically and consistently, "at the speed of light," as he put it. At some point in his development as a child he had concluded that if he could only find the holes in his life, he could fill them and would then be happy. So he was always subconsciously and automatically looking for the holes, for what was missing. Now he saw the fatal flaw in this strategy: there was *always something* missing. His life was never perfect, no matter how many holes he tried to fill. So he always found he was lacking, and this led him to feel a nearly constant longing and sadness, as well as envy of others for the happiness they seemed to possess.

This realization became the key to making his practice of mindfulness fruitful. Witnessing his sadness did nothing for him, but now he knew what he was looking for. He could catch his mind's instinctive seeking for what was missing in his life and redirect his attention to appreciating what he did have, all the good in his life. He began focusing on appreciating the little things, appreciating what was present for him in this moment. Redirecting his attention in this way, he told me, had transformed his life. For the first time, he had a handhold that kept him from falling into the familiar emotional whirlpool of sadness, longing, and envy.

In childhood, we all develop subconscious strategies for survival and safety, strategies for getting approval, love, and self-worth, and these strategies lead to patterns of attention that give rise to familiar and limiting thoughts and feelings. For instance, my own pattern is based on a subconscious belief that the world demands too much of me, that I don't have unlimited resources within me, so I must conserve resources lest I be drained or somehow obliterated. As a result, my attention spontaneously watches for intrusions (yes, like being asked to build a ramp!), and I tend toward privacy and self-sufficient freedom. To maintain my self-sufficiency, I focus on knowledge rather than feelings. This is why meditating, and developing expertise in meditation, has been second nature to me, and why my path of integration is to instead engage with others and give of myself generously.

Subconscious beliefs and patterns of attention such as these are the foundation of the personality, with its blind spots, defenses, and foibles. These adaptive patterns profoundly affect our relationships, and because the mind and body are intimately connected, the patterns also create imbalances and even illness in the physical body. Further, they create blockages in the energetic body, in the nadis and chakras, working against the clearing of the chakras that happens during meditation.

You can't change these hidden patterns by force; transformation is a gentle process. Meditation helps because it deepens your awareness, which is by nature the silent witness of all the layers of the heart and mind. This growth of inner awareness can help you become mindful of your own subconscious patterns of attention throughout the day. As I found out, however, this is not automatic; it requires consciously applying your awareness to mindfulness.

As you begin to see your underlying patterns of attention and understand how they limit you, you can consciously redirect your attention to counter what is dysfunctional. This can heal you on all levels: physically, emotionally, energetically, and spiritually. As ever, the subtle is the more powerful; changing underlying patterns of attention will cause a cascade of changes affecting your thinking, emotions, energy, and health. Whether you've known it or not, you've been living by the power of attention — it's formed your personality. Now you can become free through that same power.

Getting a handhold on your underlying beliefs, your patterns of attention, and your blind spots can be an elusive task because they are subconscious and automatic. One key is to "do the hard thing," whatever doesn't come easily to you. In my case, making meditation a priority in my life has always been second nature. Meditation fits perfectly with my subconscious belief and pattern of attention: it restores my energy and gives me bliss, knowledge, and self-sufficiency. But while meditation brings positive value to my life, overindulging my love for meditation isn't going to result in personal transformation and integration. It's not my personal evolutionary challenge. Rather, my challenge is to meditate no more than anyone else and focus on engaging with others and being as aware of their needs as I am of my own. That is what will expand my reality.

To give an example of an opposite case, my wife is naturally attentive to the needs of others. The subconscious belief she adopted in childhood says that to be loved she must be needed. As a result, her attention naturally goes to the needs of others in her hope that her own needs will be filled in return. When she walks into a room, she instantly knows who needs her help. So much does her attention go to the needs of others that she has a hard time stopping for self-care, such as meditating. Yet if she doesn't attend to herself, eventually resentment is the result. Becoming aware of her own needs, setting healthy limits on her giving in order to stay authentically in touch with herself, and making self-care a priority are her challenges. Never missing a meditation would be great for her, both for the benefits of meditation and the value of integration.

Saint John of the Cross said it well in his depiction of Mount Carmel:

> *To come to the pleasure you have not*
> *you must go by a way in which you enjoy not*
> *To come to the knowledge you have not*
> *you must go by a way in which you know not*
> *To come to the possession you have not*
> *you must go by a way in which you possess not*
> *To come to be what you are not*
> *you must go by a way in which you are not*

This, in essence, is the path to integration. So the question is, are you aware of your blind spots? What comes easily to you, and what doesn't come easily, especially in your relationships with others? (Personal blind spots and habitual patterns tend to show up most vividly in relationships, because hopefully, sooner or later, the people close to you will let you know.) In other words, what subconscious beliefs, and what underlying habitual patterns of your attention, create problems in your life? And based on that, what could you be doing to expand yourself? If you don't know, don't worry; there are tools available that can help you. I have found, for instance, the study of the Enneagram to be one such invaluable tool. The Enneagram provides a clear picture of nine fundamental personality types, each based on a unique subconscious belief and pattern of attention. Hypnotherapy is another tool I use to identify the subconscious, and often damaging, conclusions one has made about oneself and to release them. (For more information about these tools, see the Resources section.)

It is fascinating to see how these patterns of attention block not only personal growth but also the chakras, and how, by becoming mindful of these patterns of attention and countering them, you can help open your chakras and integrate higher consciousness into your personality. Such mindfulness works in concert with meditation to bring about true integration. It is an exciting challenge of personal growth, and it is gratifying to feel yourself changing and growing in ways that might otherwise have seemed impossible.

KEEPING YOUR CHAKRAS CLEAR

The following pages will give you a starting point for integrating the benefits of your meditation in terms of the chakras. There may be a number of possible patterns of attention that block a given chakra; here I will describe only the one or two most common for each chakra. Also, one pattern of attention often plays a role in blocking more than one chakra. The chakras are interrelated; they are a system and do not exist in isolation. They support one another. As you open and integrate your personality in relation to one chakra, this will pay dividends by assisting your opening and integration in relation to other chakras as well.

Root Chakra

As we discussed in chapter 3, the root chakra is the locus for the earth element in the body. Clearing and opening this chakra releases contracted instincts relating to security and survival. When this chakra is open and clear, you will naturally feel trust in life; you will feel safe and secure, and your sense of self will be well established, stable, and grounded. You will have a realistic and positive outlook on life.

When this chakra is not clear, you will experience the opposite of these feelings. In other words, you will be subject to fears, anxieties, and insecurities. You will tend to be on the lookout for what can go wrong, seeing potential hazards or threats, possibly magnifying the negative and failing to see the positive in your life. A common symptom of imbalance at this chakra is "scarcity consciousness" — focusing on lack or feeling you do not have enough.

Dynamic action, as I suggested earlier, is a great first step toward integrating the root chakra in particular. This is because a common underlying habit of attention that blocks the root chakra is the instinctive perception of hazard, which leads to doubt and ambivalence, which in turn makes taking decisive action difficult. This pattern of attention is based on the belief, developed in childhood, that the world is a dangerous and unpredictable place, which naturally directs your attention to what could go wrong.

If you are subject to this pattern of excessive caution and wariness, consciously make an effort to set aside your doubts and take action that your common sense or intellect tells you is appropriate. Not only will this offer all the benefits of dynamic action mentioned earlier, but it will also begin to free you from the underlying doubt and fear that limit you. Better yet, further counter your fears and insecurity by examining the ways in which your life is already constantly supported and nurtured by grace.

Consider all you have been given: what would you do without the air you breathe, the clean water you drink, and the delicious foods you eat that nourish you and allow your body to survive? Think of how blessed you are to have shelter and clothes, not to mention family and friends who love and support you. How blessed you are to enjoy a degree of good health, intelligence, and so on. The fact is, you are supported by grace flowing to you from all sides. Yes, there is uncertainty in life, but there is also a great deal of what the poet Wallace Stevens calls "deft beneficence." To recognize this nearly endless web of support that nurtures and protects you is to overcome fear and develop gratitude and a sense of security instead.

Such a shift in attention is the beginning of living a mature, grounded sense of security, of living a life in which you accept the inevitable uncertainties and move forward despite them. Not only will you move through your fears, but also the resulting trust will transform your life and prepare you to be an instrument of grace.

Sacral Chakra

This chakra is the locus of the water element in the body. Clearing and opening this chakra releases attachments, addictions, and the tendency to repress desires and emotions. This results in a harmonious relationship with your emotions and your sexuality. As this chakra clears, you will develop greater powers of creative expression and the ability to easily and gracefully respond with high emotional intelligence when relating with others. You will also find yourself moving and speaking in a creative flow that brings an aesthetic, almost poetic quality to your experience.

When this chakra is not clear, your life suffers from rigidity and a repression of desire, or the opposite, sexual or pleasure addiction. Your attitudes will tend to be fixed and unyielding, and your creative expression will be limited.

One possible pattern of attention that commonly blocks this chakra arises when, somewhere along the line, you learn that being good, doing things correctly, and following rules are the way to gain love and self-esteem. As a result, your attention naturally goes to right and wrong, to judging your own behavior and the behavior of others. The inner critic and judge are highly active, which means you have difficulty letting yourself be relaxed, free, and comfortable with who you are. You tend to engage in black-and-white moralistic thinking and have a hard time accepting gray areas. Losing self-control feels threatening, and so desire and sensuality are uncomfortable. Repression of desire, anger, and sensuality tend to result.

Whether or not this describes you, you can help integrate

the opening of the sacral chakra by practicing being present with and accepting all your feelings and desires. Can you appreciate the profound sacredness of all of life's pleasures, including sex? If not, what is it that blocks that appreciation in you? Be aware of any tendency to deny your feelings, desires, or natural enjoyment of pleasure. Is judgment taking place within you? If so, counter this with acceptance of and gratitude for experiences of pleasure, enjoying them in a balanced and healthy way, knowing that you deserve to enjoy them.

Another common pattern that can block the sacral chakra is a compulsive thirst for pleasure and positive experiences to protect oneself from life's pain. This habit of attention is motivated by the belief that life is limiting and frustrating and consequently painful. You believe this pain can be avoided, and so you attempt to escape limitation and potential pain by turning your attention to what brings pleasure and fun. This can lead to pleasure addiction, which blocks the sacral chakra as surely as repression of desire does. It will also block the root, navel, heart, and throat chakras, restricting your ability to trust in life, to act effectively, to feel deeply, and to find and speak your truth.

If you observe this pattern of attention arising in you, counter it by maintaining present-moment awareness, staying with what is actually happening without trying to escape. Stick with life as it is. Enjoying the experience of pleasure in a balanced and healthy way means staying present, aware of the natural flow of your life through both ups and downs, which are necessary for your growth and happiness. Practice empathy for others, for escape often means injuring others by breaking agreements and commitments. Empathy will help you honor your relationships and commitments and develop your emotional intelligence.

Navel Chakra

The navel chakra is the locus of the fire element in the body. Clearing and opening this chakra releases issues relating to personal power. This results in a genuine, expansive, secure sense of personal power characterized by acceptance and tolerance of others. When you have cleared the navel chakra, you will attract others and be a natural leader; most importantly, you will be able to accomplish your desires in the world without strain. Your personal power will shine in a balanced way that benefits yourself and others.

When this chakra is not clear, you may suffer from a lack of willpower, discipline, and confidence. You may feel weak, ineffectual, passive, and unable to manifest your desires. You may, conversely, be dominating, aggressive, manipulative, and arrogant.

One common pattern of attention that blocks the navel chakra is that of focusing on the requests, demands, and agendas of others while forgetting or putting off what is important, or should be important, to you. This pattern of inertia regarding the self arises from concluding, while still a child, that in order to get along in the world, you must blend in. In the process of accommodating others and maintaining harmony, your own priorities and sense of importance suffer. Your effectiveness, strength, and dynamism are sapped.

If you relate to this, make an effort to notice when you

sacrifice your own needs and agenda for those of others. Counter this tendency by consciously attending to what is important to you, even if it seems uncomfortable to do so. Throw yourself into addressing your own priorities.

Whether or not you can relate to the foregoing pattern of attention, to integrate the opening of the navel chakra you'll need not only dynamic action but also something else: skillful action. To act with skill is, first of all, to act with your priorities straight. This means performing needful action, action that is the natural next step in the flow of your life. Sometimes the next step is clear because of the goals you have set and are working toward. Sometimes the next step comes as a surprise, but you feel it is right — you just know it.

This raises an important point about goal-setting. Setting goals is vital, but consult your heart deeply, with an open mind. Ask yourself: are your goals based on a fanciful wish, or are they aligned with the next step presented to you by life, which is governed by the intelligence of the universe? As your mind and heart become clearer, as well as saturated with the fulfillment and ease of pure being, you will naturally discern your next step and set meaningful and intelligent goals worth achieving.

Gradually, your will and the will of the Divine become one, and so your actions gain the support of a power greater than your limited ego-mind. This is the mark of the navel chakra being wide open. Your actions become graced. They become more effective because they are aligned with nature, with life and growth. As one of my teachers put it, to act skillfully is to do less and accomplish more. The secret of this is that life is performing the action; you are just a willing, dynamic instrument.

As you integrate higher consciousness into your life, this will become your experience more and more often, until ultimately it becomes a paradox: From the outside you appear dynamically engaged in skillful action; on the inside you are steeped in the eternal silence of your innermost Self, ever beyond doing. Everything is accomplished for you by nature, and you, the essence of you, pure being, are the nondoer. This is the pinnacle of skill in action: accomplishing everything and yet doing nothing.

Another perspective on this development is that you are gaining the ability to manifest your desires from the source of creation, your own innermost Self. This does not mean you can sit and meditate and fulfill every desire. That would lead to a completely imbalanced and impractical life. The catalyst of dynamic action is still required to bring results; nonetheless, invoking the invisible support of divine grace is a great secret of skill in action.

Heart Chakra

This chakra is the locus of the air element in the body. Clearing and opening this chakra releases emotional blocks and attachments as well as selfishness and unfolds unconditional love, compassion, well-being, and devotion. When you have cleared the heart chakra, not only will your love flow to all, but also you will possess a sweetness of being that is a combination of humility and an open heart. Your emotional intelligence will become your infallible guide in life.

When this chakra is not clear, you may be withdrawn, emotionally disconnected from others, and lacking in empathy. Others may see you as living "in your head," and you may unconsciously mute your feelings. Conversely, you may experience great ups and downs in your feelings and be subject to emotional drama. You may also be jealous, clingy, and demanding in your relationships.

One pattern of attention commonly associated with a blocked heart chakra is a compulsive analytical focus by which you dampen your feelings. You may tend to withdraw from deep emotional connection because you have come to believe that life demands more than it gives and so you must preserve yourself and your energies lest you become depleted. In this way, you contract into the intellect without even knowing you are doing it. You become an observer of life and strive to maintain a comfortable privacy and isolation to ensure that you and your resources are not drained.

If you relate to this, notice your tendency to withdraw from others, from your heart and into your head. This is the signal to focus on engaging with others and engaging with your feelings. When you feel a need to preserve yourself from outside demands, stay present instead. In this moment you have all the energy you need to engage fully in your life, and in fact you will gain energy by connecting with others, by opening your heart.

This is only one of many possible patterns of attention that block the heart chakra. Another example is the pattern demonstrated by my friend who focused on what was missing in his life and so suffered frequent bouts of sadness and longing. Even though he had great access to his feelings, it was stormy emotional weather indeed. By focusing on appreciating the good in his life, he was able to calm the storms.

There are other blocking patterns, too, but whatever the pattern of attention, when the heart chakra is blocked, one element will inevitably be present, whether obvious or hidden: self-centeredness.

Self-centeredness, in some form or another, is a ubiquitous human trait, and it wears many guises. For instance, one common pattern of attention arises from a fear of rejection or abandonment, so you focus on the needs and wants of others as a means of feeling needed and staying connected. What appears selfless is actually a desperate attempt to ensure the well-being of self.

Likewise, my seemingly altruistic teenage desire to merge into the Divine was essentially a selfish desire. I was focused only on my own enlightenment. This served me for a while, because it motivated me to meditate and heal in some ways. But only after many years did I finally come to understand that this self-centered desire had set me on a course that had to be corrected. I did not have to entirely give up my desire for divine bliss; but in order to really expand beyond my ego, I did need to learn to seriously consider and support the happiness and well-being of others as well.

To develop selfless action and open your heart, focus on acting with kindness and compassion. It is hard to simply "be selfless"; selfishness is so ingrained that selflessness may at first seem an abstract and almost unattainable quality. But you can act kindly and with compassion for others, which is tangible enough. And if you do, you will automatically find yourself vitally interested in the happiness and well-being of others —

you will not only be interested, but you will also be acting on their behalf. That requires your time, energy, and resources. If that is not selfless action, what is?

To start, focus on acting with kindness and compassion at least once a day. As you get in the swing of it, see if you can make this your focus in all your interactions. If you can do this without expectation of rewards, not only will you be living your spiritual ideals, but also you'll be building a deeper, stronger sense of self that does not depend on perceived fair treatment or recognition by others. This is a powerful, albeit challenging, meditation in action that can rapidly transform your personality. Nothing is more integrating for the heart chakra than selfless, loving action.

Throat Chakra

The throat chakra is the locus of the element of space in the body. Clearing and opening this chakra releases issues relating to an inability to find and speak one's truth; this results in authentic and eloquent self-expression. You naturally stand in your highest Self, and your speech expresses the coherence of your whole being. It has the ring of truth and is naturally attractive and compelling.

When this chakra is not clear, your sense of truth will elude you. You will speak from your head and not from the core of your being. Your speech may be wily, evasive, or weak, or you may tend to dominate others verbally. Defensive arguing is a common symptom of an unclear throat chakra.

The capacity to stand in your truth and speak your truth depends first on a strong, grounded sense of Self. So integration of the root and navel chakras is an important basis for integrating and opening the throat chakra. Likewise, being able to connect with your heart is essential to knowing your truth, and a clear sacral chakra will support you in expressing yourself in easy, graceful, flowing speech, so clearing the heart and sacral chakras are also important.

We have already touched on a number of common patterns of attention. All of these — all ego strategies for surviving, for gaining love, self-regard, and acceptance — are subconscious devices that dislocate you from the truth of your being. To fully open the throat chakra, you must see your pattern, whatever it may be, understand it, and counter the dysfunctional and limiting aspects of it in order to uncover who you really are. Then you will find yourself standing in the truth of your being.

Just as self-absorption or self-centeredness always accompanies a blocked heart chakra, one trait is always present with a blocked throat chakra: defensiveness. Rare is the person who does not become defensive when criticized. That is approximately how rare it is to have an opened throat chakra. What is defensiveness but a forceful attempt to deny or block information that might actually help you grow? This verbal resistance to life both indicates a block in the throat chakra and reinforces that block, so this is one obvious entry point where you can begin to clear this chakra.

When confronted with criticism, fair or unfair, try to observe your tendency to react defensively. Hold back from blurting the first thing that comes to you and instead listen with curiosity to the other person's perspective. His or her perspective will certainly hold at least a grain of truth and possibly more. It is a precious opportunity for you to learn something about yourself, to perhaps see a blind spot of your own, an unintended consequence of your subconscious pattern of attention. Even if the critique of another person is largely unwarranted, you can resist the contraction of ego and so exercise your muscles of ego expansion by responding with openness and curiosity. Criticism is a great gift if you can remain open and nondefensive.

Simply remaining open and curious in the face of criticism will go a long way toward clearing your throat chakra, as well as your root, sacral, navel, and heart chakras. Not only will your speech be more attractive and flowing, but you will also gain a grounded, natural sense of self, reclaim your personal power, and develop a humble and open heart.

Third-Eye Chakra

The third-eye chakra is the locus for the mind. Clearing this chakra releases you from a tendency to cling to a gross material perception of life. The result is genuine spiritual vision and intuition — a clear, deep perception of the inner reality of life. This is the opening of the wisdom eye, which results in highly developed intuition, psychic abilities, evenness of vision, and deep bliss.

When this chakra is not clear, you rely on dry rationality for your worldview and reject the spiritual and intuitive levels of life. You deny the validity of your own higher Self and higher knowledge, which only robs you of the peace and happiness that is your birthright. Spiritual cynicism is an offense against the dignity of your own life, which is vast and mysterious and shining with truth. Cynicism is an attempt to squeeze the unbounded ocean of possibilities into the drop that is the range of the rational mind.

The patterns of attention most likely to contribute to blocking this chakra are those that tend toward cynicism, such as the focus on potential hazard, which we discussed in relation to the root chakra, as well as the focus on control and power, which arises from the belief that life is hard and unjust, and so one must hide one's vulnerabilities and be powerful in order to avoid being dominated.

To help open the third-eye chakra, see if you can observe when thoughts arise from the belief that life is dangerous, hard, or unjust. Counter these with an awareness of the opposite: that life is beneficent. When you observe cynical tendencies in yourself, counter these by consciously remaining open and curious. You do not have to believe everything you hear, but at least allow yourself to be open, to be in the unknown.

Keeping an open and curious mind is the first step to developing intuition. Next, tune in to your own innermost feelings. Again, don't blindly accept what others say, even if they are in positions of authority, without subjecting it to the test of your own feelings about what is right. This is not the same as cynicism; it is an act of tuning into your own intuition. If something that someone else says feels wrong to you, go deeper into your feelings to discover why. You may find your own fears or biases at the basis of your feelings, and this discovery can lead to self-knowledge and opening your mind. If cynicism is entering into your feelings — if you are shutting off possibilities because of a negative bias — consciously suspend that negativity and remain open. At the very least, identify what you do think is possible and true in the situation and try not to deny any possibility a priori. This will help you connect with a deeper, positive knowingness.

Once you do connect with your knowingness that is not based in negativity, trust it and act on it while remaining open. You are choosing to live intuitively. Meditation naturally opens you to delicate layers of consciousness that are extremely sensitive and perceptive. Practice trusting those.

One practice that helps integrate not only this chakra but also the navel, heart, and crown centers (as well as minor chakras in your hands) is energy healing. For energy healing to be effective, you must trust in your intuition and set aside thoughts arising from your rational, doubting mind (this helps open the third-eye chakra). Energy healing also trains you to become an egoless conduit for the Divine (promotes opening the crown center) and to develop the art of doing less and accomplishing more (helps clear the navel chakra). Finally, energy healing presents a wonderful opportunity to practice compassion and selfless giving. You will find your heart chakra blossoming as you become a conduit for healing love and light.

Of course, there are practical benefits, too: profound healing can take place. Just recently my wife was diagnosed with breast cancer. Both my wife and I have been trained as Reiki Masters (Reiki is a particular style of energy healing), so for ten days I practiced healing on her for about half an hour, morning and evening, while she practiced healing visualizations. At her next checkup, her doctor was amazed to report that the tumor had mysteriously disappeared. In his words: "You've been doing something...."

Though the results of energy healing can be extraordinary, the ability to become a conduit for healing love and light is entirely natural and open to anyone. If you wish to learn more, I highly recommend Reiki training (see the Resources section), which you can acquire over a few weekends. You will find it, in combination with meditation, to be a powerful means of integrating higher consciousness into your life.

Crown Center

The crown center is the locus in the body for pure awareness. Clearing this spiritual center dissolves identification with the body, mind, and ego, which keeps us in a state of separation from the world and people around us. Opening the crown center also results in an expansive and blissful realization of the Infinite, of oneness with all, enlightenment.

Before you can fully open the crown center, all your other chakras need to be mostly open and clear, which allows for the unrestricted flow of spiritual energy from the root chakra to the crown. If your first six chakras are clear, this means you are no longer rigidly bound by your adaptive patterns of attention. For the most part, you are free, a natural, unconditioned human being. In other words, you are trusting and secure, and you accept your emotions and sexuality. You are secure in your sense of self and personal power and equally accepting of others, and you possess a natural humility and an open, compassionate heart. You stand in your truth, your speech is aligned with your whole being, and you trust your well-developed intuition. As many before me have pointed out, this is not a superhuman state. It is normal and natural human life.

From here, it is only one fairly significant step to opening your crown center and gaining enlightenment: the dissolving of ego identification that separates you from others. When that boundary dissolves, you realize your oneness with all beings and all things and with the Divine.

A SIMPLE MEDITATION IN ACTION

Meditation begins to soften and melt the boundaries of ego that create separation, that make you see the world as entirely "other" than yourself. As these ego boundaries soften, you naturally begin to feel closer to others. Understanding, empathy, and love grow; you may at times feel that you are one with nature or with someone close to you. You can further this softening of ego-separation, and even tangibly experience your unity with all, by practicing the following simple meditation in action. You can perform this meditation at almost any time (*not* while driving or operating machinery, however), but I find it especially wonderful when I'm hiking in nature. At first glance it may appear somewhat complex, but it's actually fairly simple. It consists of the following steps:

1. Become aware of your own innermost Essence.
2. Become aware of the beingness that underlies all forms around you.
3. Feel the unity between your being and the beingness of all around you.

That's the essence of it; the following paragraphs offer further details to help you realize each of these three steps.

Become Aware of Your Innermost Essence

The idea is that you are seeking to directly experience your true Essence, pure awareness. Recall our discussion of pure being and your inmost Self from chapter 1. That discussion was largely an intellectual exercise in discovering the higher Self; now you will do so experientially. An easy way to do this, either during activity with eyes open, such as while walking in nature, or as an eyes-closed meditation, is by the process of elimination.

Identify any aspect of yourself that you experience. For instance, you might first notice your body. Is your body your innermost Essence? Clearly not; there is something interior to your body that is more essentially "you." So gently dismiss your body from the focus of your awareness. To gently dismiss something from your focus, you might feel something like an inner windshield wiper lightly swiping it aside from your attention. So lightly swipe aside your awareness of your body.

Continue your search for your innermost Essence. What is a more intimate aspect of you in your experience right now? You may notice, for instance, your thoughts or feelings. Certainly they are more intimate to you than your body; still, they are not your Essence, for they come and go while something else, some more intimate aspect of you, remains. So gently dismiss your thoughts and feelings from your awareness. (Even though they may still come on their own, you are not interested in them.)

Now search for what underlies your thoughts and feelings. Feel the space of awareness in which they occur. This space of awareness is abstract and subtle. What could be more subtle than this space of consciousness within you? It is the most interior aspect of you, your inmost Self.

Now, allow your conscious awareness to rest in that space of inner awareness. If you can't easily access or stay at that level, you can gently think the mantra Aham Brahmasmi (pronounced *Ahum Brahmasmee*), which means: "I am Brahman." Brahman is that grand unity within which everything — all time and space — exists. It is the same as your own Self, simple pure awareness, which is the Self of all. Think this mantra a few times, let it fade away, and then simply *be* in the inner silence of your awareness. The vibratory quality of this mantra, which is extremely powerful, will enliven your experience of that silent inner awareness.

Whenever any other thought or perception comes up within your awareness, gently dismiss it, and *be*. Even if awareness itself becomes an object of your awareness, gently dismiss it, too, for awareness is never an object but always pure subjectivity. In simply being, you *are* pure awareness. You are your Essence. You don't have to do anything to experience this. You are already there. Just be. Sometimes it may feel like a vast ocean of peace; at other times it may seem like nothing at all. Either is fine. Don't crave any particular experience. If a feeling of craving some experience comes, gently dismiss it and *be*.

Until you are able to simply *be*, you may alternate between the process of gently dismissing whatever object comes to your awareness and thinking "Aham Brahmasmi," which will open the state of pure being for you.

When you feel very comfortable with this process, you may move on to the next step. In fact, you will know when it is time to move on, because you will already have begun to spontaneously glimpse the beingness underlying everything around you. Until then, enjoy the peace and felicity of just being.

Once you feel completely comfortable with all the other aspects of Effortless Mind meditation discussed in this book, you might try this first step with your eyes closed, very innocently and effortlessly. It is a wonderfully pure and natural form of meditation that eliminates all objects of experience so that only the pure subject, or Self, remains. When you are ready for it, it beautifully opens you to the emptiness and fullness of pure being. It also further empowers your meditation by engaging more of the brain while transcending — it engages that aspect of the brain related to a subtle aspect of intellect.

How do you know if you are ready to practice it as an eyes-closed meditation? Give it a try; if it seems easy and plunges you into a profound state of being, then you are ready!

Become Aware of the Beingness That Underlies
All Forms around You

While simply being, you will have greater access to feeling the underlying beingness of everything around you. That beingness is entirely abstract. It is one with your own being. Gently put your attention on the abstract presence or beingness of all the forms around you. You may feel it, but it is really beyond feeling; it is at the level of pure being.

Feel the Unity between Your Being and the Beingness of All around You

Because your innermost being is the same as the beingness of all around you, it is relatively easy to feel your being and the beingness of the world flowing into each other, uniting. Feel that one wholeness of pure being. Your being and the being of all around you are the same. Allow your mind to dwell in that inner and outer silence and oneness. Don't think about it; rather, just dwell in that inner, silent awareness that underlies all thought. From that inner awareness, you can feel your unity with all.

If you are in nature, you might then feel your connection with the spirit of the trees, water, mountains, with all the beauty of nature. Feel the life force of nature feeding you through your senses, heart, and mind. Feel yourself in harmony with all that surrounds you. This simple awareness will nourish your spirit.

This is a powerful meditation in action that will develop the experience of unity, the hallmark of enlightenment. But don't stop with this meditation. As much as you are able, live the implications of unity consciousness. Not only see others as your own innermost Self, but also treat all beings as you would treat yourself, with love, compassion, and understanding. This is the culmination of all meditation.

As you establish your daily routine of meditating with eyes closed, put some gentle attention on these meditations in action. Especially focus on acting with kindness, compassion, and generosity and on staying open and curious. This will help to integrate the opening of all the chakras.

CONCLUSION

WHERE TO GO
FROM HERE?

You now know how to meditate. You have everything you need to successfully meditate on your own for the rest of your life. In order for you to begin to live your full creative and spiritual potential, all that remains is for you to establish a regular practice and to mindfully integrate what you gain in meditation through dynamic, skillful, and loving action. With this in mind, I'd like to share a story with you.

In the spring of 1996, I was on silent retreat high in the Himalayas. One sunny afternoon, I was meditating on the edge of a beautiful canyon. Along the floor of the canyon far below me rushed the glacial waters of the Ganges River. As I meditated, surrounded by a deserted forest, cliffs, and snow-clad peaks, a middle-aged swami walking through the forest came over to me. When he got within a few feet of me, he stopped and waited. Feeling his presence, I opened my eyes.

"Ah, meditating. Very good," he said, beaming a great smile.

I had met many of the swamis of this area, but I had not seen him before. I would have liked to speak with him, but at the time I was observing silence, so I simply nodded and smiled. He understood immediately.

"No problem," he said. "I'm just happy to see you meditating. Not enough people meditate. They don't realize that life without meditation is like a string of zeros."

I smiled. His analogy seemed a bit extreme, but I figured he meant that if you don't regularly tap your very core and connect with all you really are, your life is simply one experience after another. You are born, you live, you die, without realizing your own Self or the Divine.

"But adding meditation," he went on, "is like adding a 1 in front of all those zeros." He smiled broadly, opening his arms to indicate something huge. "Now you have a million, or a billion, or a trillion." His eyes twinkled brightly as he watched for my response.

I nodded with a smile, and he turned and walked off.

I liked this happy swami, and I never forgot his analogy. Just by daily adding the simple act of meditating — a nearly insignificant "1" — you give new significance to everything you do throughout the day. The string of zeros instantly gains great value. What was a string of life experiences now becomes the means of integration, of evolution, of transformation of a life into the light of the Divine.

No doubt you will always grow through your experiences, whether you meditate or not, but experiencing the deep waters of your own being each day helps place you in the center of the stream of your evolution, where you will travel smoothly, quickly, avoiding the rocks and sharp branches in the shallows. It will bring energy, vitality, clarity, and depth to your journey.

Whatever meditation means to you personally, I hope you do make it a regular part of your life, and that the peace and delight you receive from it sustain you, so that wherever your journey leads, it will be filled with light and love.

Enjoy!

ACKNOWLEDGMENTS

Since I first began exploring meditation in 1970, I have had many wonderful teachers to whom I owe a great debt of gratitude. These include Maharishi Mahesh Yogi, Mata Amritanandamayi, and Swami Dineshananda. Without such great, enlightened teachers, I would still be floundering, wondering how to meditate. They laid the groundwork for my further explorations, which have borne fruit as the practices throughout this book.

Thanks also to all the folks at New World Library: Jonathan Wichmann, assistant editor, and Bonita Hurd, copyeditor, for their many astute suggestions; and Marc Allen, cofounder and publisher of New World Library, who first conceived of the book, insisted that I write it, and served as an inspiring light by which I was able to steer the project safely to port.

Most importantly, thanks to my wife, Keesha, who, by her love and example, has taught me much more than I have been able to express in this book, and without whom this could never have been written.

NOTES

CHAPTER 1. WHAT IS MEDITATION?

Page 1 *The fairest thing we can experience is the mysterious*: Albert Einstein, *The World as I See It*, trans. Alan Harris (New York: Open Road Integrated Media, 2011), p. 5.

Page 6 *I have so much to accomplish today*: Quoted in Phillip Goldberg, *Roadsigns: On the Spiritual Path* (Boulder, CO: Sentient Publications, 2006), p. 262.

Page 8 *Happiness is a ball after which we run wherever it rolls*: Quoted in Otis Henry Tiffany, *Gems for the Fireside* (Tecumseh, MI: A. W. Mills, 1883), p. 806.

Page 12 *As the Katha Upanishad attests*: *Eight Upanishads, Volume 1, with the Commentary of Shankaracarya*, trans. Swami Gambhirananda (Calcutta: Advaita Ashrama, 1986), p. 145.

CHAPTER 2. PREPARING TO MEDITATE

Page 20 *In the words of Adi Shankara*: Adi Shankara, *Aparokshanubhuti: Self-Realization of Sri Sankaracharya*, trans. Swami Vimuktananda (1938; reprint, Calcutta: Advaita Ashrama, 2001), pp. 60–61.

CHAPTER 4. CHAKRA MANTRA MEDITATION

Page 41 *"In the beginning was the Word"*: John 1:1, in *The Jerusalem Bible* (Garden City, NY: Doubleday, 1968).

Page 43 *The Dhyana-Bindu Upanishad describes this*: Dhyana-Bindu Upanishad, trans. K. Narayanasvami Aiyar, verse 18, www.scribd.com /doc/50423495/Dhyana-Bindu-Upanishad, accessed July 26, 2012.

CHAPTER 5. CHAKRA MEDITATION WITH DIVINE LIGHT

Page 53 *Christ said: / "I am the light"*: John 8:12, in *The Jerusalem Bible* (Garden City, NY: Doubleday, 1968).

Page 53 *In India's most revered scripture, the Bhagavad Gita*: *The Song of God, Bhagavad-Gita*, trans. Swami Prabhavananda and Christopher Isherwood (New York: Mentor Books/New American Library, 1951), p. 112.

Page 54 *Tibetan Buddhism speaks of the essence of mind as light*: *Tibetan Yoga and Secret Doctrines*, ed. W. Y. Evans-Wentz (New York: Oxford University Press, 1969), p. 166.

Page 56 *As he put it, "Imagination is more important than knowledge"*: Albert Einstein, *Cosmic Religion: With Other Opinions and Aphorisms* (New York: Covici-Friede, 1931), p. 97.

Page 57 *In his Yoga Sutras, the primary text*: Samkhya-yogacharya Swami Hariharananda Aranya, *Yoga Philosophy of Patanjali*, trans. P. N. Mukerji (Albany: State University of New York Press, 1983), p. 105.

CHAPTER 6. CENTERED IN THE HEART

Page 70 *As Christ put it: "You will listen and listen again"*: Matthew 13:14–15, in *The Jerusalem Bible* (Garden City, NY: Doubleday, 1968).

CHAPTER 7. HEALTH AND LONG LIFE

Page 78 *in one recent study, meditation was found to significantly increase*: T. L. Jacobs, E. S. Epel, J. Lin, E. H. Blackburn, et al., "Intensive Meditation